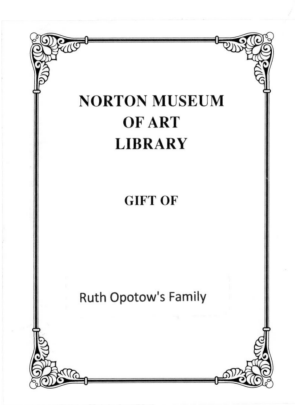

THE BERLIN MUSEUM

Paintings in the Picture Gallery, Dahlem-West Berlin

THE BERLIN MUSEUM

Paintings in the Picture Gallery,
Dahlem–West Berlin

RÜDIGER KLESSMANN

HARRY N. ABRAMS, INC. · PUBLISHERS · NEW YORK

Translated from the German by D. J. S. Thomson

STANDARD BOOK NUMBER: 8109–0037–8
LIBRARY OF CONGRESS CATALOGUE CARD NUMBER: 78–153494
© 1971 RÜDIGER KLESSMANN
TRANSLATION © 1971 THAMES AND HUDSON LTD, LONDON
Printed in West Germany
Bound in the Netherlands

CONTENTS

INTRODUCTION

In the heart of Berlin, between the Friedrichstrasse and the Alexanderplàtz, the Stadtbahn (municipal railway) passes through the 'Museum Island'. Even the express train from Paris to Warsaw winds its way between the museums, giving the passengers a fleeting glimpse of the exhibition rooms. The buildings, which are crowded together, have a somewhat sombre grandeur which must have made a rather forbidding impression on visitors to Berlin in the past, and today they will find it hard to imagine that this part of the capital once housed Germany's finest collection of art-treasures and was a centre of international research.

Today the Museum Island lies in the Eastern sector of the divided city. Some of the badly damaged buildings have been restored, while others still bear the scars of the Second World War. They have been able to accommodate only a part of the priceless collections for which they were originally designed. This unique organism was crippled not merely by the ravages of war but also by the subsequent division of the city.

For long the Museum Island had the great advantage – and could take pride in the fact – that within its confines were to be found outstanding examples of the world's great cultures. This universal collection, which had been accumulated over several generations, was no more than a torso when the war ended. The visitor can still enjoy the incomparable display of art treasures from the ancient world, from Greece, Egypt, and Asia Minor, but other departments have so far not returned to the 'Island'. The Picture and National Galleries, the collections of sculptures and engravings and the arts-and-crafts museum have, for the most part, found a new home in West Berlin. The division of Berlin runs right through the middle of the collections; their partition between East and West, which was dictated by the circumstances of evacuation and the disposition of the Allied front lines at the end of the war, has hardened into an apparently immutable status quo. For the time being the only remaining link that binds the Berlin museums together is their common history.

The Museum Island is fully entitled to its name, for it is entirely surrounded by the River Spree. From 1830, when Friedrich Schinkel built his first museum at the Lustgarten, thereby connecting the island with the adjoining palace and revealing its potentialities as a museum site, subsequent generations – in accordance with Frederick William IV's plan to 'convert the whole of the Spree island behind the museum into a sanctuary of art and science' – continued the work of development on the island with the construction of the New Museum and the National Gallery. Even when growing traffic congestion made it necessary to build railway-lines across the island, cutting clean through the site, the work continued. Around the turn of the century the fourth and most unconventional building on the island, the Kaiser-Friedrich Museum, appeared on the isolated northern tip.

For a long time Schinkel's Old Museum, which for almost 75 years had housed the Prussian art-treasures, had been unable to keep pace with the expansion of the collections, and there was a growing demand for a new building which would provide a home for the paintings and sculptures of the Christian era in particular. The building was finally completed in autumn 1904 and was named after the monarch who had died in tragic circumstances in 1888 after a reign of only 99 days. This dedication was not a mere gesture of dynastic piety, for Frederick III, as Crown Prince, had been an active and enthuasistic patron of the arts and the contribution he made to the expansion of the Prussian museums is beyond dispute.

The man who was actually responsible for creating the Kaiser-Friedrich Museum was the Director of the Picture Gallery and Sculpture Collection, Wilhelm von Bode; he was not only a distinguished art-connoisseur in many fields but also a remarkable organizer. He was a typical product of the Wilhelmine period, level-headed yet enterprising, and completely in harmony with the ideas and hierarchical system of his time because he knew how to cope with them and carry them with him in the realization of his own personal ambitions.

Both as a zealous collector and as a far-sighted scholar he felt the need to add systematically to the existing collections and to open up new perspectives, with a view to creating a complete, encyclopædic treasure-house that would include the lesser talents as well as artistic masterpieces of any given period, and would cover the whole range of pictorial art. Bode's plans were based on a wide-ranging expertise embracing not only Flemish and Dutch Baroque painting but also Italian Renaissance art, and which stimulated research into the still relatively unknown early German panel paintings. He was responsible for the almost faultless collection of masterpieces representing Dutch landscape painting in its various stages of development and for the richly varied collection of Dutch primitives – one of the finest in the world and already recognized as such before the First World War. An important part in amassing this collection was played by Bode's colleague, Max J. Friedländer, for it was he who first embarked on this particular field of research.

Bode's contribution in lending character to the Picture Gallery as a whole is apparent in the way it reflects the aesthetic tastes of his generation but it is in the choice of works that his influence is most noticeable. His conservative approach to contemporary painting was as far removed from the avant garde as from Court art. The restrained German style of Impressionism, the art of a Max Liebermann, seemed to him 'more sound, full of sensitivity and artistic effect than that of almost any other German artist of the period'. On the other hand, he could see 'no great works of art' in the pictures of Cézanne or Van Gogh. This preference for a palette with muted tones and impressionistic colours naturally influenced Bode's choice of pictures for the gallery and gave it its very special character. The substantial acquisition of late 'impressionistic' works by Rembrandt – twelve in the period 1879–1907 alone – and of similar works by Rubens and Titian is as significant as the fact that admission to the museum was denied to the ecstatic works of El Greco and other Mannerist painters.

By 1914 the Picture Gallery had reached a fairly definitive stage in its development, and at that time the collection could lay claim to being remarkably self-sufficient. But the First World War interrupted its growth; for the first time, after almost a hundred years of continuous expansion, the gallery now experienced, as a result of war reparations, a number of important losses, such as were to be suffered again later and on a much more alarming scale. Although the death of the German Empire and the birth of the Republic did not radically alter the organization and working of the museum, the economic depression which followed the Treaty of Versailles made any further expansion virtually impossible. But at least the actual buildings on the Museum Island remained untouched and this outstanding cultural research-centre continued to function.

Barely had the Kaiser-Friedrich Museum opened its doors, than it was realized that within the foreseeable future it would be unable to accommodate the steadily growing collection, particularly as, during the construction period, several rooms had been put to uses not originally intended. The huge palace façade of Mushatta, which had been acquired from Syria, also had to be housed, for the time being at least, in the new building. Although the Kaiser-Friedrich Museum had already taken many years to complete, Bode faced up to the need for further expansion. Before long he succeeded in putting into effect a particularly bold plan: the construction of an Asiatic Museum in the suburb of Dahlem, which would take the ethnological and non-European art collections together with the Mushatta façade, thereby relieving the pressure on the Museum Island and eliminating any future accommodation problems. Work on this spacious building, designed by Bruno Paul, was started in 1912 but was interrupted by the outbreak of the First World War, and even after the war it proved impracticable for the unfinished building to be used as a museum. In fact, forty years were to pass before Bode's far-sighted plans, which had long since been forgotten, could be realized in a new form – though in quite different and far from happy circumstances.

The Second World War played appalling havoc with the Berlin museums; the internal disruption and structural damage suffered by the Picture Gallery were such as no other collection of comparable stature has ever experienced. When war broke out the museums had, of course, been evacuated and the works of art stored in bunkers and mine-shafts to protect them against air-raid damage. But no one could possibly have foreseen at that time that, even several decades later, normal conditions would still not be re-established. It was not merely the destruction of the buildings that made it impossible to restore the pictures to their original home, for the division of Berlin in 1948 finally scotched any idea of moving the works of art from their West German store-rooms back to the Museum Island in the Eastern sector of the city. Hence the political situation lent even greater urgency to the need to complete the still unfinished building in Dahlem in order to provide a proper home for the art treatures which had been returned to West Berlin.

More than two decades have passed since the Dahlem Museum, containing part of the collection of pictures, was opened in autumn 1950. Several more years were to elapse before the store-rooms in West Germany could be unlocked and all the remaining pictures moved to Berlin. Even today the Picture Gallery at Dahlem can display only a limited selection, as the building, which is in itself too small, has also to accommodate the sculptures and engravings, and the ethnological departments.

Anyone visiting the Picture Gallery today will find some 500 pictures on public display; these represent only the best, for West Berlin possesses more than twice that number. The Museum Island in East Berlin is still the repository of some 900 pictures, of which, however, relatively few would survive the present rigorous selection process as the great majority had been relegated to the store-rooms even before the outbreak of war. Their absence therefore is not likely to be noted by the visitor to Dahlem; what he will miss are the masterpieces of the Kaiser-Friedrich Museum which were destroyed by fire in the Friedrichshain bunker in 1945 and only the memory of which remains. When this disaster happened in the closing days of the war, no one was capable of appreciating its true magnitude; the loss suffered can never be made good, and it has left the world a poorer place. About 400 pictures, many of them outstanding works of art, and roughly the same number of sculptures were destroyed; these works alone could have formed an impressive collection.

If, in spite of the heavy losses it has suffered, the Berlin Picture Gallery can bear comparison with collections anywhere in the world, this is due entirely to Wilhelm von Bode, who realized at an early stage how important it was to introduce system into the building-up of a museum, and who always insisted that only the best was good enough. While this latter principle is more in evidence today than ever before, one effect of the wartime losses on the collection as a whole has been to upset the balance not merely within individual schools and periods of art but even in some styles of picture. These changes will be discussed in more detail later; inevitably, however, one is constantly and painfully reminded of the greatness of the pre-war collection. The object of this book is not just to recall the past but also to provide an impression of the Picture Gallery of today; the illustrations have therefore been chosen from among the works at present on display in the Dahlem museum.

THE GREAT ELECTOR AS
ART-COLLECTOR

The origins of the Berlin Picture Gallery go back to the seventeenth century, that is to a period in which other princely capitals already possessed considerable art-collections. As the Electors of Brandenburg were relatively poor, art-collecting on a similar scale was for them virtually excluded. The first Prussian prince to engage in politico-cultural activities was Frederick William, the Great Elector, and this in spite of the strain imposed on his financial resources by the Thirty Years' War.

During his formative years this Prince of Brandenburg was given a foretaste of the heady cosmopolitan atmosphere of a Western European Court. His mother, a grand-daughter of William of Orange, had sent him to Holland, where he matriculated at Leyden University and spent several years in close proximity to the Court of the Statthalter Frederik Hendrik, at a time when that country produced an extraordinary wealth of artistic talent. It was during these years too that Rembrandt received commissions from the Statthalter. The Prince was also a frequent guest at the Court of the widowed Queen Elizabeth of Bohemia, who kept a modest establishment in exile at Rhenen but remained an active patron of the arts. In 1646, after succeeding his father as Elector, he married his cousin, Louise Henrietta of Orange, a daughter of the Statthalter, who in the same year summoned Willem van Honthorst from The Hague to Berlin as Court painter; later a considerable number of pictures came into the possession of the House of Brandenburg when her mother died. Joachim von Sandrart, author of the first German history of art, paid tribute to the Elector as a patron of the arts and in 1679 dedicated the second part of his *Teutsche Academie* to him.

No sooner had the Elector ascended the throne than he began corresponding with a wide range of ambassadors, agents and dealers, in order to augment his collection of art-treasures. His interest was by no means confined to pictures. In 1652, for example, he acquired from his cousin, Prince Johann Maurits of Nassau, a valuable Brazilian collection of pictures, drawings and books on the natural sciences, and he probably also bought the collection of drawings by Matthäus Merian the Younger, which was to form the basis of the Berlin collection of engravings. The motive behind these purchases can be partly explained by the dynastic rivalries of the period, but there was also an element of personal dedication, which is reflected in an episode recorded in contemporary documents. The Elector had seen two floral pieces by the still-life painter Daniel Seghers at the house of his Dutch brother-in-law and expressed a wish to acquire a similar picture by the same artist. He had to promise a substantial payment in kind to the Jesuit College in Antwerp, of which the artist was a member, in order to acquire the picture, a painted relief of the Madonna with a garland of flowers. This obligation he met by presenting the College with certain holy relics from Berlin Cathedral, among them two silver-mounted fingers of Saint Lawrence. However, not all the Elector's art-dealings ran such a smooth course. There is a note of concern in one letter, in which he asks an ambassador to consult an expert 'who will investigate whether these are all original . . . If, however, We could first see the pieces, this would please Us even more.'

One must assume that Frederick William was mainly interested in Netherlandish painting, with which he had become familiar during his student days. His knowledge of Italian art does not seem to have been rated very highly. In 1671 the Amsterdam art-dealer Gerard Uylenburgh tried to sell in Berlin thirteen pictures of doubtful authenticity which bore the signatures of some of Italy's greatest painters. But the Elector's Court painter Hendrik de Fromantiou declared that they were copies and had them returned to Holland. A long legal battle followed, in which many well-known Dutch painters were summoned as expert witnesses, and the final verdict went in the Elector's favour. The decisive factor seems to have been the outright rejection of the pictures by the last of the experts to be consulted: no less a person than Jan Vermeer van Delft.

A diary kept by Constantin Huygens the Younger, son of the famous poet of the same name and Secretary to the Statthalter Frederik Hendrik, contains some brief references to the Elector's collection of pictures. In October 1680 Huygens accompanied the Prince of Orange, who later became William III of England, on a visit to Berlin. In the palace there was a 'small gallery of pictorial works', which led to the Elector's private apartments and in which the pictures were apparently arranged by schools. Huygens made the critical comment that he had seen the 'majority of the Elector's paintings, which included perhaps 25 or 30 good pieces and a large number which were worthless'. The paintings in question appear to have been mainly Netherlandish. Rubens and Van Dyck are repeatedly mentioned, together with some works from the Italian Renaissance, principally by the Venetian masters. Titian's *Portrait of a Young Man* (Cat. No. 301), which Van Dyck recorded in his Italian sketch-book, is part of this collection. An attempt – following the example of other rulers – to produce a permanent record of the gallery in a series of engravings fell through due to lack of suitable talent. Although there is plenty of documentary evidence of the Elector's activities as a collector, the extent and quality of his collection is given scant attention. Descriptions of the pictures are so vague that it is seldom possible to identify any individual painting in the present collection.

THE PICTURE GALLERY
OF FREDERICK II

In 1740, half a century after the Great Elector's death, Frederick II, subsequently known as Frederick the Great, ascended the Prussian throne. The collection of pictures had grown in size during the previous decades as a result not so much of the personal enthusiasm of the rulers as of two bequests. For the most part the new additions were Netherlandish paintings which passed from the House of Orange to the House of Brandenburg, first in 1675 on the death of Amalie von Solms, wife of the Statthalter Frederik Hendrik, and in 1702 on the death of her grandson, William III of England. The pictures were selected from various Dutch palaces and transported to Berlin in several consignments; this process continued into the reign of Frederick II. The bequests included many works by minor Dutch artists, portraits of members of the House of Orange and of the English royal family, compositions by Rubens and Van Dyck, and not least two early works by Rembrandt from Frederik Hendrik's collection, *The Rape of Proserpine* and the so-called *Minerva*.

The son of the Great Elector and first King of Prussia, Frederick I (1688–1713), was more addicted to pomp and ceremony than to art. He had a picture gallery installed in the palace, in which all the pictures were uniformly framed. He added nothing of significance to the existing collection. The same is true of his successor, Frederick William I (1713–40), whose strict, puritanical nature appreciated only what was useful and inhibited any true feeling for art. It is true that he himself occasionally painted pictures, which displayed considerable naïveté, and that Dutch pictures were bought in The Hague at his instigation, but the instructions he sent to his ambassador reveal his soldierly mentality: '. . . and I will rather have many but good pieces than few and very dear ones.' He also did not think twice about exchanging parts of the Berlin collection of antiques for two regiments of dragoons from Saxony. In short his character fits perfectly the popular image of a typical Prussian monarch. His more sensitive son Frederick, on the other hand, possessed artistic qualities that did not conform at all to this pattern.

There can be little doubt that Frederick II's love of the arts was first stimulated by the conflict with his puritanical father which began in childhood.

His demonstrative interest in artistic pursuits and the devotion to French culture which was a hallmark of the Crown Prince's Court at Rheinsberg show all the signs of an attitude of protest. In the French paintings of his period, particularly in the arcadian world of Watteau and his circle, he found an echo and an intensified statement of his own view of life. As early as 1739, at the age of twenty-seven, he wrote to his sister Wilhelmina, Margravine of Bayreuth, that he had filled two rooms with pictures, most of them by Watteau and Lancret. The pictures were intended not so much for prestige purposes as to decorate his rooms, which he furnished to his own personal taste, and even after his accession the King's policy remained unchanged. The newly built royal residences in Berlin – at Charlottenburg and Potsdam – and especially the *maison de plaisance* 'Sanssouci' (completed in 1747) merely served to intensify Frederick's need to surround himself with pictures conforming to his taste. His representatives in Paris, including the Prussian Ambassador Count Rothenburg, did not find it easy to satisfy the King's wishes, particularly as he was in the habit of dictating the format of the pictures and was not prepared to pay any price. Others who acted for him were the Marquis d'Argens, author of a book on painting, the highly cultured Venetian Francesco Algarotti, who was also acting on behalf of the Dresden art collection, and naturally Frederick's Court painter Antoine Pesne, who as a member of the Paris Academy had the best possible contacts. Thus, gradually, a large collection of French paintings comprising several hundred works was amassed, the outstanding importance of which came to be recognized only much later.

Jean de Julienne, a friend of Watteau's, remarked in 1736 that there were paintings by the artist in Prussia, by which he must have meant Rheinsberg. This French collector was also at one stage the owner of a major work by Watteau, the so-called *Enseigne de Gersaint*, which Frederick succeeded in acquiring around 1745. Watteau's *Embarkation for Cythera*, another and richer version of the well-known picture in the Louvre, was also in Julienne's possession before it found its way to Potsdam. It is known to have been there from 1765 onwards. Although not all the pictures which Frederick acquired as the work of his favourite artist have stood up to expert scrutiny, there are still at least ten genuine Watteaus in Berlin today.

In the Palace of Sanssouci, in the design and construction of which the King played an influential part, some of the pictures were housed in the so-called Small Gallery, a long room with five windows facing north. Pale-green marbled walls and ornamental floral motifs in stucco combined with the symmetrically arranged pictures to create an overall impression of intimate harmony. The private character of this gallery seemed to Frederick's contemporaries somewhat eccentric, as is clear from the sarcastic reference made by the Landgravine Caroline of Hesse to the royal master of the house: 'Apparently one does not expect to see crinolines in it, for the gallery is too narrow for such.'

No other Court collection ever bore the personal stamp of the monarch as clearly as that of Frederick II. Its composition also reflects the change to a more mature artistic appreciation which he experienced in the 1750s and to which he himself applied a quotation from the poet Nicolas Boileau: 'Jeune, j'amais Ovide; vieux, j'estime Virgile.' The euphoric and entirely one-sided enthusiasm for *fêtes galantes* shown by Frederick in his youth gave way to a more mature view of life which may have been influenced by the style of other galleries such as Dresden, Düsseldorf or Salzdahlum. When he visited these art-collections in the summer of 1755 during a visit to west Germany and Holland, he must already have seen them through different eyes, for in the previous winter he replied to an offer of several paintings by Lancret with the remark: '. . . I must say that they are no longer to my taste, or rather that I have had enough of this style. At the moment I like buying works by Rubens and Van Dyck, in short pictures by the great painters, whether they be Flemish or French.' In the same year he charged his agents to look round Paris and see if 'hübsche grosse Tablau de galerie' ('pretty, large gallery pictures') by Titian, Veronese, Luca Giordano and Correggio could be bought 'vohr honete Preise' ('for honest prices').

In fact, ten years after the Palace of Sanssouci was built the King appears to have been seized by a fresh collecting passion, the fruits of which the Small Gallery was clearly no longer large enough to accommodate. Not only was a new building required to provide the necessary space, but the new style was also to be seen in its external appearance. 'The gallery which I am building is quite new,' he wrote to his sister Wilhelmina in November 1755, 'I have taken nothing from the gallery in Berlin; nevertheless I have already collected almost a hundred pictures . . .' The long, narrow building, erected on the east side of the Palace of Sanssouci, was designed in the French style by Johann Gottfried Büring; work on it began in the spring of 1755, but due to the outbreak of the Seven Years' War the building was not completed until 1764.

The interior of the picture gallery with its seventeen south-facing windows presents a cool, monumental appearance; its imposing proportions come as something of a surprise. A more striking contrast to the intimacy of the Small Gallery it would be hard to imagine. The long walls facing the windows are packed with large pictures, separated only by the pillars which support the central dome; a room adjoining the east wing is reserved for the smaller pictures. The impression of solemn dignity conveyed by this over-abundant display of pictures set against a background of dark marble is enhanced by the choice of subjects, for there are no still-lifes, no landscapes and no genre

17

The picture gallery at the Palace of Sanssouci

scenes. Frederick wanted to see only 'pieces from fable or history', but no saints or martyrs.

Making up a large proportion of the gallery's pictures were compositions of the Flemish and Italian Baroque with their conspicuously large figures. The majority of the Italian paintings (by Reni, Albani, Maratta, Cortona, Giordano, etc.) had profane subjects which were in line with the King's literary tastes. From Batoni in Rome he commissioned a *Marriage of Cupid and Psyche*, the only contemporary picture in the gallery. In his self-confessed aversion to sacred subjects he was, however, not at all consistent, particularly when he was dealing with important artists. Amongst the Flemish masters, for example, there is a marked preponderance of religious themes. Side by side with the *Holy Family* and *The Raising of Lazarus* by Rubens were three altar-paintings by Van Dyck – *Christ Crowned with Thorns*, *The Descent of the Holy Ghost* and *Saint John the Baptist and Saint John the Evangelist* – acquired by Frederick

18

in 1755 from the Abbaye des Dunes at Bruges. During the same period he purchased in Paris two major works by Rubens – *Perseus and Andromeda* (from the Pasquier Collection) and *Saint Cecilia*. The latter, one of the artist's later works, had been put up for auction in 1756 as part of the Duc de Tallard's collection, together with Domenichino's *Liberation of Saint Peter*, an outstanding example of early Roman Baroque art.

A famous painting of the Italian Cinquecento also came from the Pasquier collection to Potsdam, Correggio's *Leda and the Swan*. Its previous history alone, which the Paris agents made no attempt to conceal from the King, lent it great prestige and may well have influenced the purchase. Painted for the Emperor Charles V around 1530, the work came into the possession of the Emperor Rudolf II (1603) and, after the conquest of Prague in 1648, found its way into the collection of Queen Christina of Sweden; since 1722 it had belonged to Philip, Duke of Orleans, Regent of France following the death of Louis XIV. Dutch painting, formerly not distinguished from Flemish, was represented by only a few pictures, among them three major works by Rembrandt. The early *Samson*, theatrically menacing, which was believed at the time to represent a Dutch prince, served as a foil to a painting from the later period, the visionary figure of *Moses*. Finally there was the *Self-portrait* of 1634, showing the artist in his velvet cap and fur-collar.

In 1755/56 Frederick pressed forward with the construction of the new gallery, but soon had to turn his attention to the unwelcome events of the Seven Years' War. As noted above, he left the pictures collected by his predecessors undisturbed in Berlin Palace as he felt the need to demonstrate his own talents. In acquiring certain outstanding paintings, the royal collector undoubtedly gained a reputation for himself, but Frederick's efforts must be regarded as modest compared with those of Augustus III of Saxony, an insatiable picture-hunter who in 1745 bought the whole of the Duke of Modena's famous collection for Dresden. But whereas Augustus spared no expense where good pictures were concerned, Frederick always remained a careful and shrewd bargainer, who prided himself on seizing favourable opportunities. There is no doubt that the spectacular purchases made for Dresden wounded Frederick's pride, for he repeatedly criticized the dazzling but at the same time unscrupulous artistic policy of Augustus III, who gave twelve tons of gold for the Modena collection alone: 'The king in Poland is quite at liberty to pay thirty million ducats for a picture and to introduce a capitation tax of 100 million Reichsthaler in Saxony, but that is not my method. What I can acquire at a reasonable price I buy, but anything that is too dear I leave for the King of Poland, for I cannot create money . . .'.

In the case of the great masters such economy did not pay, as is shown for example by the unfortunate absence of Raphael from the gallery. A *Holy*

Family which was bought under his name is now attributed to Granacci, while another work, *Lot and his Daughters*, is believed to be the work of Otto van Veens. It is true to say, however, that Frederick lacked reliable advisers, so that he was all too often fobbed off with copies and works by pupils. Of the thirty-eight paintings listed in the 1771 catalogue as being by Rubens barely a quarter can, by modern standards, be attributed to the master.

It was obviously Frederick's ambition to see the heightened reputation of his Kingdom reflected in the splendour of his royal residence and to be able, like other rulers, to boast a gallery which he himself had created. The element of prestige may well have outweighed the satisfaction of acquiring expensive works at any price. How else is one to interpret his remarking in 1755, when he said that he needed another fifty pictures to complete his gallery, 'This craze for pictures will not last long with me, for as soon as I have enough, measured by the yard, I will buy nothing more.' But even when the Seven Years' War was over, leaving the Prussian State much weaker, Frederick resumed his art-purchases and in 1764, the year the building was completed, Matthias Österreich produced the gallery's first catalogue, later reissued in revised editions. Even when the collection at the gallery of Sanssouci was more or less complete, the King continued to buy paintings. Most of them were hung in the New Palace in Potsdam, a spacious building which was started immediately after the end of the Seven Years' War. In his later years, however, the King's enthusiasm for augmenting the collection seems to have waned and to have given way to a rather more contemplative frame of mind. Contemporaries report that he spent as much as four hours a day in the gallery.

There is another feature of the gallery at Sanssouci that is worth noting. The princely gallery of the Baroque period was generally one of a series of official apartments designed for ceremonial purposes, and as such was little more than a reception-room hung with pictures and forming part of the palace complex. The gallery at Potsdam was one of the first museum buildings to be constructed independently and designed solely to house pictures; it is certainly the oldest gallery extant on German soil. The idea appears to have originated in another North German Court, the now ruined palace of Duke Anton Ulrich of Brunswick (1685–1714) at Salzdahlum. As early as 1701 the Duke had a special building erected to house his considerable collection of paintings; these works were to form the nucleus of the collection now in the museum in Brunswick that bears his name. Both in its shape and in its proximity to the palace, the so-called 'Great Gallery', a long, narrow, single-storey building, bore a close resemblance to the layout at Potsdam. This close relationship between the two Courts had a historical background: Frederick had become familiar with the picture gallery at Salzdahlum as a result of several visits there with his wife, who was a niece of the Duke of Brunswick.

THE FIRST PLAN
FOR A PUBLIC MUSEUM

As a rule only Frederick's closest friends or official guests were allowed to see the royal collections. Not until the closing years of the King's reign were pupils of the Academy of Art occasionally permitted to study paintings in the royal palace in Berlin. Frederick's successor, Frederick William II, relaxed the rules still further and in 1790 officially decreed 'that the pupils of the Academy, under the guidance of one of their teachers, have free access to all our palaces, in order to have the benefit of seeing the paintings and art-objects situated therein'; and the gallery of Sanssouci was to be for artists 'what the public libraries are for scholars, namely treasures for public use'. Permission was given to 'both native and foreign artists to have open and free access to the same, to enable them to seek out for themselves those masterpieces which they wished to copy and thereby to develop their taste'.

The Academy of Arts, which entered on a remarkable period of prosperity under the new ruler, provided the necessary intellectual climate for the realization of the first plan for a public museum in Berlin. In 1796 the archaeologist Alois Hirt (1759–1837) was summoned from Italy, where he had been working for several years, to teach the theory of art at the Academy in Berlin. The following year, in a public lecture to celebrate the King's birthday, he outlined his plan for a public museum in Berlin, in which the finest specimens of the Prussian art-treasures would be housed under one roof. 'An essential point would be the internal disposition of the exhibits: namely, to arrange the works of art in clearly defined periods and schools. Only by such a systematic classification will it be possible for the artist and art-lover to find his way through the labyrinth of art-history and to distinguish the special character of each period, of each school and of each master.'

Frederick William II immediately accepted Hirt's proposal and asked that suitable works of art should be selected for the museum, for which a plan was to be drawn up and submitted. The project 'to assemble in one single place everything beautiful and masterly that the Fatherland possesses' also had the approval of Frederick William III, who ascended the throne only a few weeks after Hirt had given his lecture. It is true that, in view of the war with France, the King wanted to delay the actual construction of the museum until the return of more normal times, but a provisional plan for the Institute was nevertheless to be worked out. By September 1798 Hirt was able to submit a design for the building and detailed proposals for the internal arrangement and organization.

A detached rectangular building with a large inner courtyard was to be erected in Unter den Linden near the Arsenal, on the spot where the 'Neue Wache' designed by Friedrich Schinkel stands today. The exterior of the museum, as shown on the plan, was reminiscent of a palazzo in the Palladian style. The ground floor was designed as a museum of antiquities, the first floor as a picture gallery. Each of the wings contained two parallel suites of rooms without corridors. The larger rooms formed the main frontage, while the adjacent rooms where the small pictures were to be hung overlooked the courtyard. Hirt planned the lighting of the rooms with great care. Each of the high windows was to be fitted with four shutters: 'By closing the lower shutters and leaving open only the upper ones, a light-effect can be created such as one finds in an artist's studio.' Hirt emphasized the importance of hanging the pictures in historical sequences, a system which until then had been applied only in the imperial gallery at Vienna. 'A gallery must be regarded as a school for the cultivation of taste; and a logical order in the display of works of art is the first essential for any gallery.'

Hirt's 1798 plan is a unique document in the history of European museums. Even though circumstances prevented it at first from being realized or further developed, it nevertheless helped to promote the construction of the later museum and had an influence on its overall design. Three years later, when Hirt recalled his plan, which was 'so important for the advancement of artistic taste', Napoleon's spectacular victories were already arousing widespread concern for the security of the State. The crushing defeat which Prussia suffered in 1806, Napoleon's entry into Berlin and the severe economic burdens imposed by the Treaty of Tilsit finally pushed the project completely into the background; however it was not forgotten. The publisher and engraver Christian von Mechel, a friend of Winckelmann's, who had reorganized the Vienna gallery several years before at the request of the Emperor Joseph II, in 1781 introduced a new system there which Hirt described as the finest in Europe. Mechel, who had become a member of the Berlin Academy of Art in 1806, was entrusted with the reorganization of the gallery at Sanssouci which the French had plundered, and it was he who reminded Frederick William III once again in 1810 of the project to create in Berlin 'a public and carefully selected art-collection'. The King did at least give instructions that a complete inventory of the works of art in the various palaces should be drawn up, and when completed it comprised 2,244 pictures; the State's finances were, however, in no condition to permit any building to be done.

22

In 1806 Vivant Denon came to Berlin as a member of Napoleon's suite to
select works of art for the Imperial Museum which he directed in Paris, and
to arrange for them to be transported; for this reason the French officers
referred to him as 'notre Voleur à la suite de la Grande Armée'. Denon was
an outstanding scholar and one of the leading art-connoisseurs of his time,
whom history had provided with a unique opportunity to realize his dream
of the ideal museum. This personal achievement earned him – despite the
violent circumstances surrounding it – the admiration of the whole of Europe.
By modern standards his choice of paintings from Prussian palaces – when
compared with the works plundered from the galleries in Brunswick and
Cassel – cannot be regarded as very damaging. He was obviously interested

above all in the works of early German painters, among them Lucas Cranach the Younger's *Fountain of Youth* and Baldung's late work *Caritas*. Apart from lesser works from the Italian, Flemish and Dutch Baroque, the most notable pictures he selected at Sanssouci were Correggio's *Leda* and Rembrandt's *Samson*. A petition presented by the Berlin Academy to the Emperor, requesting that the decision to remove the works of art be rescinded by him, was rejected.

The success of the Wars of Liberation and the final overthrow of Napoleon in 1815 also marked a crucial point in the history of the museum. Within a short time a wave of patriotic enthusiasm had created a new climate in which the long-delayed plan for a public art-collection became a practical possibility. On 4 October 1815, barely three months after the victorious armies of Blücher and Wellington had entered Paris, an exhibition was opened at the Berlin Academy in which paintings and works of art, which Napoleon had looted and 'which had been recovered thanks to the valour of the troops of the Fatherland', were exhibited, the proceeds going to the war-wounded. For the first time people of all walks of life had an opportunity to admire works of art which until then had been housed in various royal palaces, inaccessible to the general public. 'May they never again be separated,' wrote Hirt in a commentary on the exhibition, for which he had also compiled the catalogue, 'but continue to form a complete whole, as in other capitals. Time has taught us many a lesson, and we have become more convinced than ever that science and art must combine with military glory to give a people a true sense of national pride.' Hirt's thoughts were in accord with the idealistic principles which a Prussian Minister, Freiherr von Altenstein, had incorporated in a memorandum concerning the reorganization of the State following the defeat of 1806: 'If it is the aim of the State to enable the human race to share the best things in life, then it can only be done through the fine arts and sciences.'

On 18 November 1815, barely four weeks after returning to his capital, Frederick William III gave orders for the mews of the Academy building in Unter den Linden to be extended with a view to creating a museum. The King's sudden decision to put into immediate effect the museum project for which Hirt had battled in vain for years is rather surprising, for it cannot be attributed solely to the euphoria of victory and the knowledge that the country had been freed from the crushing burden of enemy occupation. There is no doubt that he King had also been influenced by his stay in Paris during the peace negotiations. Here he had the opportunity to acquaint himself with the museum which had existed in the Louvre since the 1790s; the museum, in which a large number of works selected and brought back from countries conquered by Napoleon were assembled, had, since the

24

coronation, borne the Emperor's name. The tremendous impression made throughout Europe by this quite unique and ideal collection cannot be exaggerated; so strong was it that the violence and illegality of the methods employed to amass this wealth tended to be overlooked. What impressed contemporaries was not really the range and variety of the works on display but the obvious educational function which the Louvre had assumed since the Revolution and which provided an ideological and cultural justification for acts of vandalism. In 1794, for example, one chronicler had written: 'France will possess incalculable means to increase human knowledge and to perfect civilization.' Everyone, regardless of class, had free access to the Louvre; four days a week were reserved for artists, the weekends for other visitors. The pictures were arranged in schools and were explained in simple terms comprehensible to all; printed catalogues were also provided for the guidance and edification of the visitor. Contemporary reports speak of large crowds visiting the museum on a scale never known before, with the result that one could scarcely see the pictures for dust.

Gustav Friedrich Waagen, who later became Director of the Berlin Gallery, visited Paris in 1814; he then described the Louvre as 'a treasure-house of works of art of the highest rank, such as had never been exhibited in recent times'. He went on to say: 'Various painters, who as creative artists dominate their whole period, are so comprehensively represented that one can follow their careers from beginning to end and in the most varied expressions of their genius.' The indelible impression left on visitors to this ideal museum produced astonishing results even in the political field. When, after the fall of Napoleon, the victorious allies concluded the first Treaty of Paris in the spring of 1814, they specifically renounced the right to have all the looted art-treasures restored to their legal owners, on the ground that the people of France should not be punished for the Emperor's misdeeds. Not surprisingly, this magnanimous decision did not meet with widespread approval in the countries which were directly affected. Hence, after Waterloo and the second Treaty of Paris in 1815, the Musée Napoléon was immediately liquidated, and the works of art there, which had for some years contributed to the education of the people of France, now became once again the responsibility of their rightful owners.

The exhibition of the repatriated works of art in the Unter den Linden Academy gave the citizens of Berlin their first opportunity to see, in tangible form, the basis of a projected public museum. The King himself visited the Academy and, according to Gottfried Schadow, 'walked amongst the people, unrecognized by many'. The idea of converting the Academy building itself into a museum had already been considered by Hirt in his proposals of 1798, but without reaching any definite conclusion. In fact, when the reconstruction work ordered by the King got under way in 1816 the results were not encouraging, and finally both plans and costs had to be revised. Many years later, when still more money had been wasted, the King was finally persuaded of the need for a completely new building which, it should be noted, was designed by one of the finest architects of the period.

THE GALLERY IN THE MUSEUM
AT THE LUSTGARTEN

Friedrich Schinkel, Professor of Architecture in Berlin, had since 1816 been engaged on city planning primarily concerned with the organization of the waterways. In this context he realized that it would be possible, by filling in a canal on the north side of the Lustgarten, to create an imposing building-site and thereby to complete the architectonic design of the most important public square in the city by enclosing it on its only remaining open side. The proximity of the Cathedral and the Royal Palace, the latter with its particularly fine Baroque façade by Andreas Schlüter, demanded for the site a major civic building with a high standard of architectural design. That Schinkel had the temerity to suggest a museum for this spacious and highly desirable site, and succeeded in getting his proposal accepted, is an indication of the spirit of idealism which prevailed during this period and of the great architect's powers of persuasion.

Frederick William III seems to have immediately recognized the significance of the new project and its advantages for the city. He gave his approval without delay, and on 30 April 1823 Schinkel was commissioned to build the museum. Due to difficulties with the terrain, the foundation-stone was laid only two years later. During the period of construction Schinkel travelled widely in 1826 in order to compare notes with museums in Rome, Paris and London. Admittedly none of these collections had a building specially designed for it. In London, Sir Robert Smirke had just completed the British Museum, but in character and functional design it was more in the nature of a library. The National Gallery was still housed in the private residence of John Julius Angerstein, 100 Pall Mall, which had been open to the public since 1824. Here Schinkel met Edward Solly, whose important collection of pictures had been acquired a few years before by the Prussian State but had been placed in storage till the new building in Berlin was finished.

On 3 August 1830, Frederick William III's sixtieth birthday, the museum finally opened its doors, and the citizens of Berlin had their first general view of the treasures assembled over the years. Schinkel's building, known today as the Altes Museum (Old Museum), consists of a two-storey block, rectangular in plan. In the centre is a rotunda flanked by two inner courtyards. After

Friedrich Schinkel.
Engraving by
L. Sichling.

(Right) The south
front of the Old
Museum

passing through the entrance-hall and mounting the double staircase, the
visitor enters the stately domed rotunda, which is intended to make him
'receptive and to induce the right state of mind to enjoy and to appreciate
what the building as a whole has to offer' (Schinkel). Along the entire length
of the south front, facing the palace, runs a row of massive columns which
integrates the two storeys. The ground floor contained the museum of
antiquities, the upper floor the picture gallery. This arrangement, as well as
the comparatively small display sections lit by windows looking on to the
street-front and the inner courtyards, recalls the plan drawn up by Hirt
in 1798.

Schinkel arranged his rooms in suites by setting up partitions, thus pre-
serving the impression of space and distance but at the same time ensuring
that the pictures always received 'the best side-lighting from the large, wide

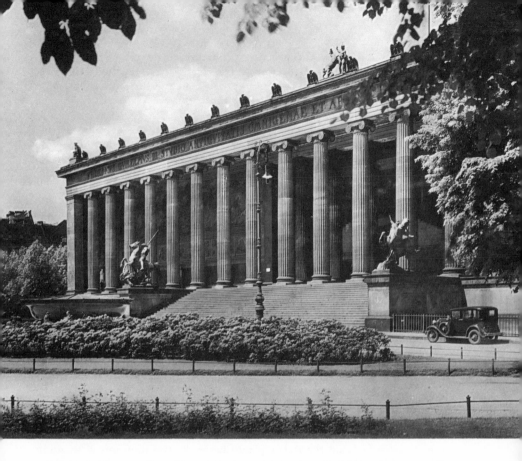

windows'. He saw that this particular arrangement had the advantage of
increasing hanging-space, facilitating the grouping of works by schools, and
enabling the visitor to view them 'in peace in a small and comfortable space';
moreover, hanging the pictures on wooden walls had the further advantage
of helping to preserve them. The walls were uniformly covered in dark red
tapestry, the ceilings were in yellow, red and white, and the structural com-
ponents, including those of the dividing walls, were gilded. Schinkel had
realized, when he visited the Pitti Palace in Florence, 'that pictures are never
displayed to finer advantage than on a rich, red ground', as they give an
impression of greater depth and space when viewed against a bold background.

The building at the Lustgarten represents a landmark in the history of
European museums: its comprehensive modern design made it the first
of its kind, and it paved the way for the great museums built in the decades

that followed to house Europe's major collections (Munich, Alte Pinakothek 1836; London, National Gallery 1838; Dresden 1855). Its functional role as an integral part of the city and its impressive architectural design together helped to establish the reputation of the comparatively recently formed Prussian art-collection.

Since 1820 Hirt had been busy selecting suitable works of art for the future museum. Schinkel and, later on, Dr Waagen helped him, but before long fundamental differences of opinion began to emerge. On the one hand, Schinkel's design for the building gave the museum quite a different dimension, on the other hand the acquisition of the Solly Collection (1821) had substantially increased the total number of pictures to be housed. Waagen and Schinkel finally decided that they must record their disagreement with Hirt in a memorandum (1828) which also reflected the difference in outlook of their respective generations. Whereas the 69-year-old Hirt represented the fundamentally scientific, classical approach to art of the eighteenth century, the authors of the memorandum took the view that the main objective must be to arouse in the general public an appreciation of the fine arts and that all other considerations, even the interests of artists and art-connoisseurs, must be subordinated to this. Only through beauty could the cultural education of the nation be promoted or indeed true education be made accessible to the lower classes of human society. In effect, the memorandum demanded – and in this it was in line with the views of the eminent art-historian Carl Friedrich von Rumohr – that only first-class original works should be selected and pictures of predominantly historical or antiquarian significance should be limited to a few examples only.

The gap had become too wide to be bridged. In spring 1829, a year before the museum was opened, Hirt resigned. After having laboured for some thirty years to bring the museum into being, he was now forced to admit that his ideas were behind the times. Hirt's functions were taken over by a newly appointed 'Commission for the Establishment of the Museum', which included, apart from Waagen and Schinkel, the sculptor Christian Rauch, the painters Heinrich Dähling and Carl Wilhelm Wach, and the restorer Jacob Schlesinger; it had as chairman Wilhelm von Humboldt. The total number of pictures from which the Commission had to make their selection for the museum was, of course, much greater than it had been when Hirt drew up his first plan. The purchase of two important collections of paintings in the meantime represented a substantial addition to the original supply in the royal palaces. The names of the two men responsible for forming these collections are still closely associated with their pictures: Vincenzo Giustiniani and Edward Solly.

THE GIUSTINIANI COLLECTION

In November 1815, a few months after the Battle of Waterloo, the Prussian government bought from the art-dealer Bonnemaison a collection of paintings formerly owned by the Marchese Vincenzo Giustiniani (1564–1637) of Rome, and at the time on exhibition in Paris. The King's attention had been drawn to this collection, which had only recently left Italy, while he was in Paris for the peace negotiations the year before.

Vincenzo Giustiniani and his brother Benedetto, who became a Cardinal in 1586, had begun collecting in Rome early in the seventeenth century. As Vincenzo survived his brother by seventeen years, it was he who gave the collection its special character, comprising, as it did, outstanding examples of the various trends in contemporary Roman painting. During the first two decades of the century the collectors showed particular interest in the new realism of Caravaggio and his followers (Baglione, Terbrugghen, Baburen, Honthorst, Regnieri, Vouet) as well as in the art of the Carracci and their school. Later, Vincenzo's interest lay rather in the more traditional works of the painters of northern Europe. He enjoyed the company of artists and sometimes acted as host to them. Joachim von Sandrart was one of those who stayed at his palazzo while arranging the publication of a book of engravings concerned with Giustiniani's collection of antiques.

The two collectors were admirably placed to follow Caravaggio's work for the Contarelli Chapel in S. Luigi dei Francesi, for the Palazzo Giustiniani was next to the church. This accounts for Caravaggio's original version of the St Matthew Altarpiece, which was rejected by those who had commissioned it as being too realistic, having found its way into their collection. Later they acquired four more pictures by the same artist: *The Agony in the Garden*, *Doubting Thomas*, *Love Victorious* and a female portrait.

The Giustiniani Collection was the first acquisition by the Prussian State for the public museum in Berlin. This particular purchase was surprising, in that the main works in the collection were in keeping neither with the taste of the period, nor with the demands of those who had initiated the museum for classical works by great masters. The art of Caravaggio and his followers, which by present-day standards constitutes one of the highlights of the collection, was regarded as unrefined when compared with the leading works of the Renaissance. The few Cinquecento pictures – including works by Lorenzo Lotto and Paolo Veronese, and some which quite falsely bore the names of Raphael and Michelangelo – can scarcely have inspired the purchase. It is not known who influenced the King in his decision nor why he was persuaded to agree. On the other hand, the price of the 157 pictures was 540,000 francs and, after the collapse of France, the franc was not worth a great deal.

It is hardly surprising that this acquisition did not arouse much enthusiasm, especially after the collection had been publicly exhibited in Berlin in 1826. The main criticism was the absence of classical masters and the large number of 'second-rate works'; indeed the painters classified in the latter category were only to achieve proper recognition a century later. In 1830 less than half the Roman collection was displayed in the picture gallery of the museum at the Lustgarten; the remainder were used to adorn the palaces.

Should anyone seek today to give an account of the high quality of this collection, in which early Roman Baroque painting was represented on a scale unknown elsewhere north of the Alps, he would in effect be writing an obituary, for it was precisely this collection that suffered most in the disaster in the Friedrichshain bunker in 1945: of the five Caravaggios only two, including *Love Victorious*, escaped destruction. Reni's great altar-picture with the hermits Paul and Anthony, Simon Vouet's early *Annunciation* and Claude Lorrain's *Landscape with Diana and Hippolytus* were also among the works lost in the fire.

In the Academy's exhibition of 1826 the Giustiniani Collection was shown together with some individual acquisitions which, according to the now very rare catalogue, 'were purchased partly in Paris, partly here'. These are the first purchases known to have been made for the museum itself. They include Luca Cambiaso's *Caritas*, Annibale Carracci's famous river-landscape and Carlo Dolci's *St John the Evangelist*; especially worth noting among the works by North European painters are the two portraits of the Emperor Charles V and the cosmographer Sebastian Münster by Christoph Amberger, and Gerard Terborch's so-called *Paternal Admonition*.

By and large, however, the purchases made for the future museum appear to have been of entire collections, because on the one hand there was always a chance of getting more favourable terms, and on the other, replicas and copies (which today would be rejected) were also acceptable. Moreover the lavish display of treasures in the Musée Napoléon and the crowds they had attracted may well have acted as an incentive to create similar art-collections in Berlin on a bigger scale than had seemed conceivable before the Wars of Liberation.

On his return journey from Paris to Berlin in November 1815 – the same month in which the purchase of the Giustiniani Collection was completed – the Prussian Minister of Culture, Freiherr von Altenstein, visited the brothers Sulpiz and Melchior Boisserée in Heidelberg. With their friend Johann Baptist Bertram, they were the joint-owners of an important collection of early German and Netherlandish paintings. Altenstein hoped to persuade the two brothers to sell the pictures to Berlin, especially as the Rhineland had in the meantime become a Prussian province. Acting on Altenstein's behalf, Friedrich Schinkel conducted the negotiations with enthusiasm and great skill, enlisting in the process the support of Goethe. As the collectors were reluctant to part with their property, a preliminary contract was drawn up whereby the owners would move to Berlin with all the works of art and would occupy a building placed at their disposal by the State. In addition to the purchase price of 200,000 gulden, they were to be given an annuity; a special fund was also to be set up to supplement the collection.

Schinkel, who had suggested the Monbijou Palace as a suitable home for the collection, pressed for an early conclusion of the negotiations in view of 'the weight of public opinion and the widespread interest in this matter'. There was indeed no shortage of generous offers from Vienna, Munich, Frankfurt, as well as from Württemberg, Baden and even Russia, so that there was no time to be lost. Schinkel made an impassioned plea to the responsible authorities in Berlin to acquire for Prussia this unique collection, the like of which 'is unlikely ever to be available again anywhere else in so complete a state'; he not only stressed the justification for providing the necessary funds, but further argued that Prussia had a cultural responsibility to its Rhine province and even pointed to the political advantage to be derived from the fact that 'Prussia is no longer regarded either abroad or within its own frontiers as a mere financial and military state'. All his efforts were, however, in vain. The Finance Minister refused to give his approval on the grounds that there were artistic (!) objections and thereby identified himself with the very image of Prussia which Schinkel had been so anxious to erase. In 1827 the Boisserée Collection was bought by Ludwig I of Bavaria and shortly afterwards was handed over to the Pinakothek in Munich.

THE SOLLY COLLECTION

For the creation of the nucleus – the royal art-treasures apart – of the collection at the Berlin Picture Gallery and the importance of the works it contained, credit must go to a man not of princely but of bourgeois origin: a man, whose accomplishments won him the respect and admiration of Berlin and whose love of art and collecting zeal set a standard which later generations continued to recognize. Edward Solly (1776–1848), an English merchant resident in Berlin, was junior partner in the London firm of Isaac Solly & Sons which specialized in the Baltic trade. He was responsible for the export of shipbuilding timber and other commodities from Prussia to England and had at his disposal a fleet of ships which was large enough to be taken into account in the planning of Prussia's defence strategy. His good work in maintaining diplomatic relations with England and in connection with the defence of Danzig elicited appreciative comment.

During Napoleon's Continental blockade Solly managed to amass a large fortune, but his interests were not confined to commerce. He was also the author of several publications on political economy and took issue with German authors over the image of England conveyed in their writings. His real passion, however, was for paintings. Solly lived with his family in a house in the Wilhelmstrasse and over the years he filled it with a range of works quite exceptional among private collections. More than 3,000 paintings – mainly by Italian masters – were arranged systematically by schools in the rooms of his house. Despite the size of the collection, he always regarded the quality of the paintings as of primary importance. Solly had acquired his knowledge of art, and certainly also his discerning eye for the Italian masters, in the Louvre and at Dresden. The Italian schools – from the earliest works to Raphael, whose complete mastery he admired – appealed particularly to Solly, and he sought to show their historical development in his collection. Napoleon's political machinations and the secularization of many ecclesiastical foundations had created no little disturbance among Italy's art-collections. Solly employed agents to trace the provenance of paintings, and showed a marked preference for works from churches and academies, as in these cases attribution was easier to check. Only after an advisory committee, which comprised the finest connoisseurs in Berlin including both Rumohr and Waagen, had recorded a favourable verdict, did Solly finally decide to make a purchase.

Even more surprising than the extent of his collection was the fact that Solly made it his aim to include the works of the Trecento and Quattrocento as historical precursors of the High Renaissance. The rediscovery of the Italian 'Primitives' was a consequence of the Romantic movement which began in the late eighteenth century, particularly in England. Worth noting are the names of Ignace Hugford (1703–78) and William Young Ottley (1771–1836), who were among the first collectors to specialize in Italian art of the Quattrocento and earlier. In Berlin, Solly's ardour must at first have been regarded as a form of eccentricity, for how else can one explain the fact that the largest private collection in Prussia is barely mentioned in contemporary literature. Similarly the early German paintings collected by the brothers Boisserée failed to arouse any response from the authorities in Berlin. One is reminded, in fact, of the words of Frederick William III, who in 1815 warned against allowing a preference for early works to be carried too far, 'for we might move backwards instead of forwards'.

In addition to Italian pictures Solly also purchased quite a number of early German and Netherlandish paintings, always with the same keen eye for quality, but it is open to question whether they were so close to his heart, for, on the few occasions when he referred to his activities as a collector, he never mentioned these schools. Just how low German painting was rated at that time can be judged from the fact that Holbein's now famous *Portrait of the Merchant Georg Gisze* remained for a long time in Switzerland without finding a buyer until, around 1810, Solly bought it for sixty guineas. Even so, the German Renaissance painters, particularly Dürer, of course, were better understood than the medieval artists. With astonishing foresight Solly realized that the Romantic movement had awakened an interest in the early German masters and he added to his collection several outstanding works from the fourteenth and fifteenth centuries, of which the panels by the Master of the Darmstadt Passion and the Master of the Life of the Virgin deserve special mention.

Solly's outstanding acquisition, however, was the Ghent Altarpiece (painted on both sides) by the brothers Van Eyck, which he acquired in 1818 from the art-dealer Nieuwenhuys for 100,000 francs. Other important works included the *Portrait of Charles the Bold* by Rogier van der Weyden, the *Portrait of a Young Lady* by Petrus Christus, two altar-wings by Jacques Darets from Arras, Gerard David's great *Crucifixion*, Jan Gossaert's masterly *Virgin and Child*, together with almost life-sized nudes by the same painter, Patinir's highly imaginative *Rest on the Flight into Egypt*, Pieter Aertsen's *Christ Carrying*

35

the Cross with its many figures, and – on the threshold of the new century – the two monumental altar-panels by Marten de Vos.

Among the Italian works the Trecento panels form only a small group, but again – another indication of the high standard set by the collector – there is no shortage of famous names (Giotto, Taddeo Gaddi, Bernardo Daddi, Allegretto Nuzi, Lippo Memmi, Pietro Lorenzetti). The main feature of the collection, however, was the Quattrocento masters, who are so widely represented that it would be pointless to enumerate them. Among the outstanding works are Fra Filippo Lippi's *Madonna in the Wood* from the chapel of the Palazzo Medici-Riccardi in Florence, Castagno's *Assumption*, Piero del Pollaiuolo's *Annunciation*, Botticelli's *Saint Sebastian*, Mantegna's *Presentation of Christ in the Temple*, Ercole Roberti's picture for the high altar of S. Lazzaro in Ferrara, Carpaccio's *Ordination of Saint Stephen*, Giovanni Bellini's *Dead Christ* and Cima's *Virgin Enthroned with four Saints*. Important Cinquecento works had become scarce even in Solly's time: outstanding among the works he acquired were an early Raphael *Madonna*, a *Resurrection of Christ* from the school of Leonardo, Titian's late *Self-portrait*, Paris Bordone's altar-painting from Belluno, Lorenzo Lotto's *Christ taking leave of his Mother*, and Savoldo's *Venetian Lady*.

There were no works by French or Spanish painters in Solly's collection, nor did it feature artists from his native England. Even the Flemish and Dutch Baroque painters, who enjoyed a considerable reputation at that time, were only sparsely represented. The collector openly admitted that he regarded the latter merely as chattels which served also to satisfy his own personal tastes; among them, however, was one important Dutch masterpiece, Rembrandt's *Jacob wrestling with the Angel*.

It is conceivable that Solly bought German works in order to make his collection in Berlin – with an eventual sale in mind – more attractive. As Solly's advisers were also the founders of the museum, they cannot have been entirely indifferent to the fate of the collection, particularly after their efforts to acquire the Boisserée Collection had failed in 1817. Waagen certainly made no secret of his concern that Solly might one day remove to England the wings of Van Eyck's Ghent Altarpiece, which had been in Berlin since 1818 and which was the finest of all the Dutch paintings he had acquired. Yet the close relations which Solly had with Prussia's leading intellectuals and with members of the government, particularly with Altenstein, the Minister of Culture, make it unlikely that he seriously intended to remove his collection from Berlin. In Berlin he could count on the keen interest of his friends in the future of the collection; and the brothers Boisserée had learned from experience how difficult it was to sell a collection that was not in keeping with the taste of the period.

36

Edward Solly. Drawing by Wilhelm Hensel, 1838. *New National Gallery, Berlin*

No sooner had the euphoria over Napoleon's downfall died down and freedom of movement been restored on the high seas, than Solly's business suffered a marked decline. The economic advantages of the Continental blockade had exacted a high price; no less than twenty ships of his fleet which Napoleon had seized in Danish waters had to be written off, complete with their cargoes. Solly hoped that Prussia and England, which had both benefited by the risks he had taken, would compensate him but the hope was not fulfilled.

Finally in 1818 he was in such financial straits that he felt obliged to offer his collection for sale to the Prussian government. At this particular time the State's finances were also in a parlous condition, so that the government did not dare spend substantial sums on works of art. On the other hand, if the English merchant were to go bankrupt, the consequences for Prussia's trade could be serious; so, as an interim measure, Solly was granted a credit of 200,000 thalers in exchange for which, however, he had to mortgage his collection. It was agreed that the final purchase-price should be the subject of further negotiation, as 'the present moment is not propitious for such an acquisition'. The principle at stake was whether the State was justified in buying works of art at a time when 'in several districts the King's subjects are in such dire need that they cannot even buy the salt for the enjoyment of their potatoes'; there followed a period of considerable discord and interminable discussions within the government, which lasted until 1821. In the meantime Solly had reached the end of his tether: unable to repay the credit he had received, he had lost his freedom as a trader vis-à-vis the State. As both sides feared an imminent financial catastrophe, he accepted a purchase price of 500,000 thalers for nearly 900 pictures. After a further payment of 130,000 thalers the Solly Collection, comprising altogether some 3,000 paintings, passed into the possession of Prussia.

The fact that sums of this size could be found was due to the insight and diplomatic skill of Chancellor von Hardenberg. Convinced that the collection would contribute to the 'edification of the people', he, together with Altenstein, the Minister of Culture, strongly supported its purchase and naturally had the backing of all Berlin art-connoisseurs. The King decided, however, that the financial arrangements should be handled with great discretion, in order not to antagonize public opinion. Although the sums eventually paid in 1821 were substantially below the original asking price, Solly himself left Berlin without rancour and returned to London the same year, while continuing to maintain friendly contacts with his adopted country, Prussia. His personal feelings towards Prussia had been expressed in a letter dated 13 September 1821 to Chancellor Hardenberg: 'It has never been my intention to bargain with this collection, and, as my sole concern and object in making sacrifices has been to ensure that the whole of it may be found a home in Berlin, I accept whatever price His Majesty may think fit to name.'

The purchase of the Solly Collection caused a sensation far beyond the frontiers of Prussia and met with the approval of the overwhelming majority of art-connoisseurs. Goethe, who had not actually seen the collection but had received an expert opinion from his friend Heinrich Meyer, welcomed the purchase, as he had 'always heard only the most favourable reports of it'. The Boisserée brothers were angered and their pride was hurt, for it had been suggested to them from Berlin that Solly's collection should be amalgamated with theirs – an idea that smacked more of idealism that of realism. Later, in 1836, the Parliamentary Committee in London which had voiced its criticism of the National Gallery's purchasing policy invited Solly to give it a detailed account of his activities as a collector in Berlin.

In the summer of 1823 Solly's house in the Wilhelmstrasse had to be vacated. Hirt, Schinkel and Waagen had taken on the difficult task of classifying, cataloguing and distributing the enormous stock of pictures: 677 works of the finest quality were selected for the museum, and 538 for the royal palaces to replace the paintings that had been removed to the Picture Gallery. The remainder, about three-fifths of the total, were put into storage.

The works from the Solly Collection selected for the museum were included in the first catalogue of the Berlin Picture Gallery issued by Waagen in 1830 for the opening of the museum at the Lustgarten. These pictures, which at that time represented rather more than half of the total on display, set a standard for the subsequent development of the gallery which earned it an international reputation in the field of early Italian and Netherlandish painting.

THE WAAGEN ERA

In August 1830, three weeks after the opening of the museum at the Lust-garten, Wilhelm von Humboldt, Minister of State and Chairman of the Commission for the Establishment of the Museum, submitted the first detailed report to the King; in this he summarized all that had happened so far and outlined a plan for the organization of the museum and a programme for its future development. Humboldt's basic principles for the functioning of a public museum are among the best ever to have been formulated; they also reflect the change of attitude that had taken place among art-connoisseurs in Berlin and those who had first launched the idea of a museum. 'A great many galleries, perhaps even all the well-known ones,' wrote Humboldt, 'can only be regarded as aggregates which came together gradually and without any specific plan. By contrast the Royal Gallery here is different in that it covers systematically all periods of painting and provides a visual history of art from its beginnings. This privileged position it owes to the Solly Collection, and it is to the eternal credit of Hofrath Hirt that he recognized this at an early stage . . . and urgently recommended the purchase of this collection. It was this that gave the gallery its distinctive character.'

Although there was full acknowledgement of the services Hirt had rendered in building up the Picture Gallery, it is clear from the tenor of Humboldt's report that it accepts the principles formulated by Hirt's critics led by Rumohr, Schinkel and Waagen. For them quality was the first and essential criterion for the choice of works. The demand for original works followed logically from this, so that copies, which Hirt had included for the museum as a matter of course, were now rejected.

Never before had the selection and classification of pictures in a museum been undertaken with such care, and the Berlin Gallery could count itself fortunate that Carl Friedrich von Rumohr, whom Alexander von Humboldt described as 'one of the greatest connoisseurs of painting of our time', took over this work, together with his pupil Gustav Friedrich Waagen. Rumohr, a dedicated art-historian, was not tied in any official capacity to the museum and was not even an official member of the advisory commission. It was the first time in museum history that a scheme for a picture gallery intended for

40

the use of the public was planned and implemented by art-historians; the major problem confronting them was to make it aesthetically satisfying while forfeiting neither historical perspective nor systematic organization. Rumohr decided that the less important, but historically interesting, pictures should be hung in the smaller side-rooms leading off the main galleries since he was of the opinion that no visitor 'should feel as it were obliged to look at them in passing, for not everyone has the curiosity or the inclination to devote serious attention to such works.'

While this more academic collection was designed for the connoisseur, the amateur would be able to recognize in the sequence of the main galleries 'the essential progression of the history of art'. Rumohr was therefore anxious that works of the German and Italian collections should be juxtaposed at the point where the schools had had any mutual contact that was 'decisive for the development of art'. That Van Eyck's Ghent Altarpiece was displayed next to works by Antonello da Messina he regarded as uniquely advantageous, for only in this way could one demonstrate that the 'school represented by the latter, which has come to be commonly known simply as Venetian, acquired not only the technique of oil-painting but also and more particularly its naturalistic tendency, from the early Netherlanders'; it was therefore essential to bring Antonello, Bellini and 'any other works of related trend and style closer to the Ghent painter Van Eyck'. Crivelli and Vivarini, on the other hand, he regarded as 'less tasty morsels' and their works were therefore consigned to the side-rooms.

Thanks to the rich variety of the Giustiniani Collection, the early Italian Baroque, the epoch of Caravaggio and the Carracci with its contrasting trends, could be graphically displayed. Moreover, Rumohr wanted to 'bring together in one department the "ideal landscapes" of all nations', on the one hand because these had originated in the school of the Carracci, on the other because he felt that the eye needed a certain relaxation after the uncompromising realism of the figure-paintings.

So influenced was the Berlin Museum Commission by Rumohr's ideas that they were adopted in almost every detail when Schinkel's building was constructed. Furthermore, the art-historical aspect was emphasized by the expedient of hanging the principal works in prominent positions – with the less important works grouped around them in order of relevance – to underline their role as landmarks in the overall development, and further distinguishing them by specially designed frames.

This was a complete departure from the eighteenth-century method of arranging pictures decoratively and, for the most part, according to subject. Never before had anyone succeeded in formulating and implementing so clearly the functions and aims of a collection. In 1830, when the museum at the

Lustgarten opened its doors, Berlin became the first city to possess a systematically organized picture gallery in the modern sense.

Rumohr not only left his personal stamp on the gallery as such but was also responsible for acquiring a number of important works. In his report to the King in 1830 Wilhelm von Humboldt mentioned that the gallery now consisted of 1,198 paintings, '346 of which came from the Royal Palaces, 677 from the Solly Collection, 73 from the Giustiniani Collection', and that of the 102 individual purchases 39 were made by Rumohr. As an outstanding connoisseur of Italian painting he frequently travelled on the King's behalf to buy Cinquecento paintings and redress the imbalance created by the preponderance of Quattrocento masters in the Solly Collection. Even at that time this was no easy task and Rumohr did not in fact succeed in substantially changing the general tenor of the Italian collection in favour of the classical painters. Nevertheless Berlin had every reason to feel satisfied: among Rumohr's acquisitions were Botticelli's *Virgin enthroned with two Saints* from S. Spirito in Florence, Piero di Cosimo's *Venus, Mars and Cupid*, once owned by Vasari, a *Portrait of a Young Girl* attributed to Lorenzo di Credi, and Franciabigio's *Portrait of a Young Man*. Two works by Raphael had previously been bought in Italy, the Colonna Madonna in 1827, the *Madonna with two Saints* in 1829; these acquisitions, however praiseworthy, are subject to the reservation that, the Solly Madonna being already in the museum, the master's earliest period in Urbino was now represented by three pictures on the same theme.

The Commission led by Humboldt was naturally anxious to retain for the museum the expert knowledge and services of this outstanding man, who was not prepared to sacrifice his independence. However, repeated pleas to the King that Rumohr should be appointed to the directorship of the gallery were turned down without any reason being given. The Commission, having completed its task, was wound up in 1831 and Waagen, then thirty-seven years of age, became Director of the Picture Gallery. Rumohr himself actively supported the appointment, for in the long run he would have found it difficult to reconcile the independent way of life of a rich nobleman with the duties which Waagen, a man of humble origins, now assumed as a Prussian official.

The son of a relatively unknown painter in Hamburg, Waagen studied the history of art at the Universities of Breslau and Heidelberg and was therefore one of the first trained art-historians to enter the museum profession. The services which this modest scholar rendered to the Berlin Museum have never met with as much acclaim as his brilliant writings – his famous book on England's art-collections deserves a special mention – and his undisputed reputation as a leading connoisseur of painting. At the same time, the purchases

Carl Friedrich von Rumohr, drawing by K. C. Vogel von Vogelstein (1828).
Staatliche Kunstsammlungen, Dresden

Waagen made for the gallery, which were cloaked under the anonymity of his office, were no less important than Rumohr's.

Waagen also took the view that every effort must be made to acquire for the gallery the greatest masters of the finest period of art, the Cinquecento, so

43

long as they remained insufficiently represented. As early as 1832 he succeeded in acquiring Titian's *Girl with a Bowl of Fruit*, believed to be a portrait of his daughter Lavinia, and shortly afterwards one of Andrea del Sarto's major works, the *Madonna Enthroned with Saints*.

Frederick William IV, who as Crown Prince had earlier formed a close friendship with Rumohr, gave his full support. When he ascended the throne in 1840, he sent Waagen to Italy and approved a special fund for the completion of the gallery. Among the fruits of this journey were Moretto's altar-painting *Mary and Elizabeth in Glory*, a series of mythological works by Tintoretto and Veronese from the Fondaco dei Tedeschi in Venice, and Tintoretto's *Virgin and Child on the Crescent Moon*. Finally negotiations were begun – though not finalized until 1854 – for the purchase of Raphael's *Madonna Terranuova*. The gallery thus acquired one of this artist's outstanding works.

As Spanish painting was entirely unrepresented in Berlin, Waagen set out to make good this deficiency, although he did not rate his chances of breaking into this market very highly, 'considering the passionate interest of the English in the Spanish school'. Nevertheless, in addition to lesser works by Campaña, Morales, Coello and Cano, he succeeded in obtaining two important paintings for the gallery: Zurbarán's *Presentation from the Life of St Bonaventure* and Murillo's *St Anthony of Padua*. Both these works perished in the Second World War.

The small number of Netherlandish paintings from the Solly Collection, of which the Ghent Altarpiece was the plum, were supplemented by Waagen to an extent that would be inconceivable today. Outstanding are the two altar-wings by Petrus Christus, two panels of the Dirk Bouts altar from the church of St Peter in Louvain and no less than three triptychs by Rogier van der Weyden, among them the Middelburg or Bladelin Altarpiece.

Whereas these were all major works, early German painting was represented for the most part only by lesser artists, and there was nothing at all by the greatest master, Albrecht Dürer. A famous altar-painting bearing his signature, the *Festival of the Rosary* from the Strahov Collection in Prague, came up for sale in 1836. As it was in poor condition, however, Waagen decided not to make an offer.

The Dutch paintings, which had come almost entirely from the royal palaces, were also supplemented by new acquisitions. Ten works by Rembrandt and a number of works by his disciples were joined for the first time by those of another major figure in Dutch art, Frans Hals, four of whose portraits were purchased. By 1843 the number of paintings bought by Waagen had reached 104 and they were then introduced into the gallery, replacing 121 of the paintings originally exhibited.

Gustav Friedrich Waagen. Engraving by C. Steckmest.
Staatliche Museen (Kupferstichkabinett), Berlin

From the 1850s onwards few purchases were made, mainly because of differences of opinion within the administration. During this period Waagen travelled abroad fairly frequently and paid several lengthy visits to England where he collected material for his famous book *Treasures of Art in Great*

Britain, which was translated by Lady Eastlake, wife of the Director of the National Gallery. As an outstanding art-connoisseur who had a wide circle of acquaintances among British collectors and connoisseurs, he was also called upon to organize large exhibitions, of which one in Manchester in 1857 was particularly successful. Waagen's death in 1868, on a journey to Copenhagen, occurred seven years after that of Frederick William IV, and marked the end of the first period in the history of the Berlin Museum, an era which was still deeply rooted in the world of German Romanticism.

THE BODE ERA

Following Waagen's death Julius Meyer became Director of the Picture Gallery, and four years later, in 1872, Wilhelm Bode, who was himself to succeed to the directorship and to become the second of the Picture Gallery's great directors, entered the museum service. The intervening years were, however, marked by profound historical changes. During this time Prussia succeeded in convincing the German federal states of its claim to leadership and, following the victory over France in 1871, founded the German Empire. The new resources of power over which Prussia now had control, and not least the high indemnities which France had to pay as the price of defeat, resulted in an unprecedented economic boom which also brought a new prosperity to the Imperial capital, Berlin. With it came a significant change in the status of the museum, which was reflected in the appointment of Crown Prince Frederick as its patron; it was now required to fill the role of a national institution, a notion quite alien to Waagen's generation. For Waagen, born as he was in the eighteenth century and a contemporary of the painter Carl Philipp Fohr, the museum had always been essentially a cultural centre such as he had first witnessed in 1814 at the Louvre.

Compared with Waagen, that humble scholar who was at once an international authority and a poorly paid Prussian official, Bode was a typical product of the period that followed the Franco-Prussian war. Financially independent and self-assured, coolly calculating and aggressively tough with himself and others, he was at once an art-historian of international stature and a man of enterprise. Social life meant nothing to him, for he regarded it merely as a waste of time, and yet he was proud of enjoying the favour and recognition of the Emperor, which he exploited by means of cunning intrigues for his own ends. It is hardly surprising that, in his all too subjective reminiscences, Bode showed little understanding for Waagen – a very different type of man – and even tried to minimize his achievements, reproaching him for not having made the most of his good relations with England by buying pictures for Berlin on favourable terms. In fact this does not seem to have crossed Waagen's mind, although the National Gallery in London on more than one occasion upset his negotiations in Italy and, in competition for any particularly desirable picture, generally came out on top.

For Bode too the National Gallery was and remained his keenest competitor, especially in the field of Italian art. From 1872, in collaboration with the Director of the gallery, Julius Meyer, he began by turning his attention southwards in search, like his predecessors, of the masters who it was felt were still inadequately represented in Berlin, the great painters of the Cinquecento. But although the budget had been increased almost tenfold, Bode's efforts fell far short of the target, whereas the Quattrocento collection acquired several more valuable additions, including Signorelli's famous painting *Pan, God of Nature*. Berlin came very near to acquiring one of Giorgione's finest works, which is now in the Accademia in Venice; the purchase of the picture known as *The Tempest* from the Manfrin Collection had actually been finalized, but at the last moment a ban was placed on its export. By a remarkable stroke of good fortune the gallery was able to acquire a portrait by the same artist almost twenty years later. Although in 1878 two important Cinquecento pictures were bought from the Palazzo Strozzi in Florence, namely Titian's graceful *Portrait of a Daughter of Roberto Strozzi* and Bronzino's *Portrait of Ugolino Martelli*, to which was added later (1885) the fine *Portrait of a Young Roman Lady* by Sebastiano del Piombo from the Marlborough Collection at Blenheim, Meyer still complained resignedly that 'the time seems to be past for such acquisitions and in this respect the present may well have to abandon all hope of making good the shortcomings of previous centuries.'

Nevertheless, thanks to Bode's outstanding expertise, the range of the Italian paintings from the Solly Collection was further extended. Particularly worth noting are two fine predellas from the Pisa Altarpiece by Masaccio acquired in 1880, which were joined twenty-five years later by four panels with figures of saints from the same altar. The portraiture of the Quattrocento was handsomely represented by the addition of two works (acquired in 1875 and 1878) by Botticelli, one by Signorelli (1894) and one by Domenico Veneziano (1897). Several additions were also made to the Solly group of large altar-paintings: Crivelli's *Virgin enthroned with seven Saints* (1892), Giovanni Bellini's *Resurrection* from S. Michele di Murano (1903), Bartolommeo Montagna's *Risen Christ with Saints* from S. Lorenzo in Vicenza (1903), and Carpaccio's mystical *Entombment of Christ* (1905). Bode was also anxious to augment the small stock of Trecento masters. He was able to acquire several panels of the high altar painted by Ugolino da Siena for S. Croce in Florence (1904–06), a small *Entombment of Christ* by Simone Martini (1904), and a large altar triptych painted by Bernardo Daddi of the Florentine school (1906).

48

Wilhelm von Bode

The political situation in Spain in the 1870s was such that there seemed a possibility of acquiring at least some, if not all, of the paintings in the Prado. It was the Minister of Finance himself who had this ill-conceived idea and who declared his readiness to make available up to fifty million pesetas for a part purchase. But all concerned, including Bode, found the proposal distasteful and it was therefore put to the Chancellor, Bismarck. It is the only occasion on which the name of this famous statesman, who took no interest in the fine arts, appears in the history of the Berlin museums. Bode recalled that Bismarck categorically rejected any move in this direction. Even if the Spanish government in its hour of need had responded to such an offer, the

Spanish nation would never have forgiven the Germans and would always have regarded the deal as a form of robbery.

Efforts to extend the range of Netherlandish paintings were highly successful. In 1874 the largest private collection in Germany, that of the industrialist Barthold Suermondt, was purchased; this was the gallery's most spectacular single acquisition since Solly's days. That the handsome price – which admittedly also included the purchase of a fine collection of drawings – of one million gold marks negotiated by Meyer was approved by Parliament was due in no small measure to the backing of Crown Prince Frederick, who proved himself an effective patron. It is difficult to understand today why Bode should have tried on various occasions to cast doubt on the value of this acquisition for the Berlin museum and to argue that its importance was overrated. This judgment, which was undoubtedly prejudiced, may be partly explained by the fact that Bode did not like Suermondt and played very little part in negotiating the purchase of his collection. Almost ten years earlier the National Gallery in London had acquired from the same collector a picture of *Christ Blessing Children*, which was attributed at that time to Rembrandt but is now believed to be by Nicolaes Maes.

Particularly prominent in Suermondt's collection, apart from important works by early German and Netherlandish painters, such as the *Madonna and Child in a Church* by Jan van Eyck and paintings by Altdorfer, Baldung and Holbein, were exceptionally fine examples of classical Dutch painting which introduced an entirely new note into the existing collection, most of which had originated in the royal palaces. No fewer than five paintings by Frans Hals, including the so-called *Nurse with a Child*, the *Singing Boy with a Flute* and the famous *Malle Babbe* now made their appearance, together with five portraits by Terborch, two works by Jan Steen and, last but not least, the magnificent *Young Lady with a Pearl Necklace* by Jan Vermeer. There were also excellent examples of landscapes by Hercules Seghers, Jacob van Ruisdael, Aert van der Neer, Adriaen van de Velde, Paulus Potter and Philips Wouwerman. These painters served to complement the impressive groups of twelve Rembrandts already in the museum and formed the backbone of the numerous works by minor masters and pupils which had been collected in Waagen's time, partly by purchases from the Reimer Collection (1843).

The extent of the Dutch collection could now be compared favourably with that of any other gallery. Yet for Bode this was only the beginning and a constant challenge to seek even greater perfection. As a north German he had a particular weakness for the art of the Netherlands and, although his interests were catholic, it never lost its special appeal for him. The next few years saw further major acquisitions, among them the interior by Pieter de Hooch known as *The Mother* (1876), the *Portrait of Tyman Oosdorp* from

Frans Hals' later period (1877) and Rembrandt's *Portrait of Hendrickje Stoffels* (1879).

Bode became more and more absorbed in the work of the great Amsterdam master. With characteristic enthusiasm and single-mindedness he set out to display in the gallery every phase of the painter's development and his range of themes. The portrait of Hendrickje was the first of a splendid series of thirteen Rembrandts which he acquired for the museum; in 1883 alone he purchased *Susannah and the Elders, Joseph and Potiphar's Wife* and *The Vision of Daniel*. But Bode's proudest achievement was undoubtedly the purchase in England in 1894 of the large double portrait, *The Mennonite Preacher Anslo*. As he later recalled, the previous owner, Lord Ashburnham, at the time asked him to prove the seriousness of his intentions by selecting a lesser work from his collection and paying for it immediately in cash. Bode chose the *Portrait of a Young Lady in Profile* attributed to Domenico Veneziano, which is today one of the best-known paintings in the gallery. It seems scarcely credible that this episode took place only eighty years ago.

As critical evaluation became more discriminating the number of genuine Flemish Baroque paintings – which had come mainly from the palaces – showed a progressive decline as copies and works by pupils were sifted out. The Suermondt Collection had brought three sketches by Rubens, a head-study by Van Dyck and a landscape by Adriaen Brouwer, but examples of large compositions, which alone could do full justice to the Flemish masters, were notably absent.

With the acquisition of Rubens' *Martyrdom of Saint Sebastian*, which the artist himself in a letter of 1618 had rated among 'the finest of my things', Bode added to the original collection an important work from the early period; this was followed two years later, in 1881, by an early Rubens composition on a mythological subject, *Neptune and Amphitrite*, from the Schönborn Collection in Vienna. One of the master's late works, which served as a profane complement to the *Saint Cecilia* acquired by Frederick the Great, was *Perseus and Andromeda*, acquired from the Duke of Marlborough's collection in 1885. From the same collection came the large *Bacchanale* by Van Dyck, which was one of the irretrievable losses suffered during the Second World War. Both pictures from Blenheim Palace, together with two others by Sebastiano del Piombo and Joos van Cleve, were bought at very reasonable prices because the subject-matter had caused offence in England. In Berlin, on the other hand, it was the splendidly exotic *Neptune and Amphitrite* from Vienna which brought protest from the established painters who were unfamiliar with Rubens' early style and, misled by its academic polish, maintained that it was a modern forgery. Bode, with his remarkable expertise, had no difficulty in establishing the work's seventeenth-century provenance.

51

A gallery in the Old Museum, showing panels from the Ghent Altarpiece, *c.* 1881–4. From a painting by Bennewitz von Loefen. *Staatliche Museen, Berlin*

The palace galleries and the Giustiniani Collection had provided a small but very good nucleus of French Baroque painting. In 1873 the three Poussins were joined by a fourth, the magnificent *Landscape with Saint Matthew and the Angel.* Claude Lorrain's *Landscape with Diana and Hippolytus*, an early work formerly in the Giustiniani Collection, was joined in 1880 by another of his works, a coastal landscape with shepherds dated 1642.

The French painters of the eighteenth century were poorly represented in the Picture Gallery, when one considers the treasures available in Frederick the Great's palaces. When Hirt and his colleagues chose pictures from the palaces for the museum the masters of the *fêtes galantes* were despised, and no one wanted to see the 'age of decadence' represented. Nevertheless, in 1830 at least two small examples of Watteau's art (Comedy, French and Italian style), together with a shepherd's scene by Lancret, were moved from the picture gallery of Sanssouci into the museum.

From the beginning Bode was determined to rectify this faulty evaluation of fifty years earlier and to arrange for a fresh and up-to-date assessment of the palace collections, applying new critical standards even to works of earlier periods. Meyer and Bode together chose some sixty pictures for the museum and their selection had the full approval and support of Crown Prince Frederick, who had been present in person during the inspection of all the palace rooms. The Court officials, however, who were concerned to preserve the palace interiors in an appropriately formal state, succeeded in holding up the proceedings whenever a fresh move was made on behalf of the museums. Hence only a few specially selected pictures were actually transferred to the Picture Gallery, among them Watteau's unfinished *Garden Party* (from Sanssouci in 1889) and a late work by Rubens, *Diana Bathing* (from the Berlin Palace in 1903).

The large number of new acquisitions soon made it necessary to cast a critical eye over the contents of the Picture Gallery itself, as Waagen had done several decades earlier, in order to weed out lesser works and make room for the more important pictures. Moreover, in the 1870s work had been started on a thoroughgoing reconstruction of the exhibition rooms with a view to introducing skylights, which had been completely lacking, and improving the ventilation. In 1880, on the fiftieth anniversary of the museum, the refurbished exhibition rooms were opened to the public.

The German department, which at that time was relatively small, had some outstanding examples of the early period on show, including two thirteenth-century altarpieces acquired from the Wiesenkirche in Soest in 1862, and several important paintings from the German Renaissance by Lucas Cranach the Elder, Altdorfer, Kulmbach, Baldung, Burgkmair and Hans Holbein the Younger. On the other hand, there was not a single picture by Albrecht Dürer. Among Bode's most remarkable achievements was his purchase of seven paintings by this great German master between 1882 and 1899, particularly as four of them were in British collections. To some extent the *Madonna of the Siskin*, which he acquired from Newbattle Abbey near Edinburgh in 1892, made up for the Strahov *Festival of the Rosary*, which was close to it in style but which Waagen had decided not to buy fifty years earlier; both works originated in Venice in 1506. A no less important work, painted in Germany, was the *Portrait of Hieronymus Holzschuher*, which had remained in the possession of the sitter's family until 1884, when it was purchased from them. The *Portrait of Jacob Muffel*, which was bought in

53

Paris, had been in the Schönborn Collection in Pommersfelden until 1867, when it was put up for sale; Waagen had then made an unsuccessful offer for it.

The great winged altars, which – thanks to the artistic taste of the Electors of Bavaria and to the dissolution of the monasteries – are today among the most prized possessions of the Munich Pinakothek, seldom changed owners even in Bode's time. As the centres of German Renaissance painting lay outside Prussia's frontiers, there was little the country itself could offer to satisfy the demands of the museum for new acquisitions, especially as the artistic treasures of the Rhine Province available to collectors had earlier been garnered by the Boisserée brothers and eventually found their way to Munich. In the Prussian provinces, however, there were still to be discovered medieval works capable of gracing the museum in the capital. Among these were the two exquisite retables from Soest in Westphalia and the huge altarpanel in the form of a clover-leaf from Quedlinburg, all dating from the thirteenth century, and the magnificent *Virgin and Child Enthroned*, a major work of the Bohemian school (*c.* 1350), from the Augustinian monastery at Glatz in Silesia. But these were the exceptions and in fact – by contrast with Munich – the greater part of the early German collection consisted of individual purchases, a state of affairs that is still apparent from the preponderance of smaller pictures and the large proportion of portraits.

The collection of Netherlandish works, which had already gained a high reputation under Waagen, was soon to prove itself superior to that of any other gallery. To Jan van Eyck's *Madonna and Child in a Church* from the Suermondt Collection Bode was able to add two portraits by the same painter, of Giovanni Arnolfini (1886) and Baudouin de Lannoy (1902); the *Christ on the Cross*, which was purchased in 1897, is clearly of a somewhat earlier date and has been attributed by some to Jan's elder brother, Hubert van Eyck. A rarity of this period was Aelbert van Ouwater's *Raising of Lazarus*, bought in Genoa in 1889; the painting had been mentioned by Carel van Mander as early as 1604 and could thus be positively identified as the work of this artist. Following the marked increase in the size of this particular collection, the Ghent Altarpiece was exhibited in an entirely novel way: in 1894, with the aid of a specially designed veneer saw, the panels were split in two in order to display simultaneously the paintings on both back and front. This dangerous operation, carried out in an atmosphere of considerable suspense, took some time to complete; Bode, who was travelling abroad at the time, arranged for news to be sent to Florence so that he might be kept informed of the progress and successful outcome of the operation.

54

THE KAISER-FRIEDRICH MUSEUM

For some years before he retired as Director of the Picture Gallery Julius Meyer had been in poor health, leaving Bode in effective control. Bode's influence in the purchase of new pictures had certainly been decisive, and the size of the collection had so increased in the 1880s, as a result of his almost feverish enthusiasm, that it was no longer possible to make long-term plans for its display in the museum at the Lustgarten. An attempt was made to provide more space and better lighting by means of structural alterations, but in July 1883, before the work was completed, a competition was organized with the object of inviting suggestions for further building on the Museum Island.

The task confronting the candidates, which Bode described as a competition for students of architecture, was extraordinarily difficult: the need for exhibition space called for maximum exploitation of the site which, however, was traversed by the municipal railway, dividing it in the most unfortunate way. These factors may explain, at least in part, why there were only fifty-two entries, some of which were quite fantastic. The most original plan was undoubtedly that of Baurath Orth, who proposed to build an enormous terrace over the railway; on this terrace would be erected, some 150 ft above ground level, the Pergamon Altar as a landmark dominating the city of Berlin.

The judges were all agreed that the northern tip of the island, cut off as it was by the railway, was a suitable site for the so-called Renaissance Museum. This building was to accommodate both paintings and sculptures of the Christian era. On the site south of the railway the New Museum (1843–59) and the National Gallery (1867–76) had already been built in the immediately preceding decades, the former for the Kupferstichkabinett (Collection of Engravings), the collection of casts and the Egyptian and Near Eastern antiquities, the latter for contemporary art.

Owing to the serious illness of the Crown Prince, patron of the museums, and the tragic circumstances of his death only three months after ascending the throne in 1888, more than ten years were to elapse before plans for further building on the Museum Island came up for discussion again. Finally, in 1896, it was decided to start work on the projected Renaissance Museum, which was henceforward to bear the name of the late Emperor Frederick, and to allocate five million marks in the State budget for this purpose. At the express wish of the Emperor William II, the architect Ernst von Ihne was commissioned to design the museum.

The ceremonial opening of the new building by William II in 1904 – on 18 October, his late father's birthday – was conducted in an atmosphere of Imperial splendour. An equestrian statue in memory of the deceased monarch was unveiled in front of the main entrance. 'To a fanfare of trumpets,' ran the official report, 'the solemn procession made its way up the grand staircase to the so-called Basilica, where leading officials of the Imperial and State governments, the Army and the Navy, together with the other guests attending at the command of the Emperor, were already assembled.' In his speech the Emperor took the opportunity, 'with regard to the prince of peace in whose honour today's celebration is being held', to pay tribute to the military successes of his late father, that 'great-hearted warrior who [as Crown Prince] fought his royal father's battles'; he seemed to regard it as more important to laud Frederick's 'Siegfried image' than his part in the creation of the most important art collection in the Empire. There was hardly any mention either of the man who first conceived the idea of the Kaiser-Friedrich Museum, who supervised its planning and execution from first to last and who had even acquired a substantial number of the works of art it now contained. For Bode, who was suffering from a leg-complaint and had to attend the ceremony in a wheel-chair, a handshake from the Emperor was recognition enough.

Bode had realized from the outset that, both architecturally and spatially, the museum presented almost insuperable problems. The site, surrounded by two branches of the river and bordered on the land side by the railway-bridge, made a triangular building inevitable. Despite this, von Ihne found a solution remarkably convincing in its way, and one which has been unjustly denigrated.

A stone base rising out of the water carries a series of gigantic columns and pilasters, which integrate the two floors and provide the substructure for the domes that crown the building. The uniformity of the exterior, which is broken only by corner projections, gives an impression of truly monumental proportions. Architecturally, it is modelled on the Italian Renaissance and North German Baroque. The sculptural décor of the building has a historical orientation and reflects the intellectual background of the Bode era. Above the entrance are six allegorical figures representing the various arts, with Painting and Sculpture placed centrally. On the projecting gables appear the coats of arms of important centres of the arts. In the middle of the huge

56

domed space – decorated in white, gold and reddish stucco – which incorporates both entrance-hall and staircase, the visitor is confronted by the monumental equestrian statue of the Great Elector, a specially made copy of the original of 1703 by Andreas Schlüter. Each of the four pillars supporting the dome is decorated on its inner surface with the eagle of Brandenburg and with medallions portraying the rulers who were patrons of the Prussian collections.

While the statue of the Great Elector, as the founder of the Picture Gallery, dominates the centre of the entrance-hall, the second and smaller staircase is dedicated to Frederick II, who did more than any other Prussian king to promote the arts. Accordingly the circular well of the staircase, with its coloured stucco decoration, reproduces motifs from the rococo palaces at Potsdam. The two famous sculptures which flank the elegant flight of stairs, Pigalle's *Venus* and *Mercury*, were brought from the Palace of Sanssouci. In the large wall-niches, alternating with pilasters, stand marble statues, by Schadow and his pupils, of six of Frederick's generals with their king in the centre; these had formerly graced the Wilhelmsplatz.

The figures decorating the two staircases were acquired and arranged *ad hoc* by Bode, who had employed the same method with the exhibition rooms in

The Kaiser Friedrich Museum, with the equestrian statue of the Emperor Frederick. The building is now known as the Bode Museum

the museum, and in his memoirs he proudly recalls how successful it was. There is no doubt, however, that the 'monumental decoration' of these rooms creates something of a conflict in the mind of the visitor today. The symbolism of the décor seems too contrived and the motifs are repeated in a way that is aesthetically questionable. The proximity of the two more than life-size equestrian statues in front of and inside the building robs each individual work of its effect. The fact that the Emperor Frederick in the role of victorious general is shown straining towards the main doorway was criticized when the museum was opened as lacking 'an inner bond between the Emperor and the ideal place'. The same is true of the well of the small staircase devoted to Frederick; here the association of the broadsword of the Seven Years' War with examples of garden sculpture from the Palace of Sanssouci is somewhat contrived.

In his desire to create the right historical milieu for each work of art, Bode achieved some astonishing aesthetic effects. While this was perhaps less convincing in the stairways and in rooms which were primarily representative in character, Bode invented a 'Berlin style' of his own in the exhibition rooms. His Italian interiors in particular, with their delicate blending of colour and material and their harmonious arrangement of pictures and sculptures, frames and chests, have been widely admired and frequently imitated. 'We had no desire,' he wrote, 'to model ourselves on some arts-and-crafts museums, but our aim in employing such monumental fittings was to give the works of art a modern setting, which would heighten their effect and correspond as closely as possible to the original intention. Had we merely reproduced old rooms, we would have lessened the monumental effect of the works of art and impaired the character and significance of the museums.' So the problem was to strike a fine balance between the reconstruction of a historical milieu and the creation of an up-to-date setting for works of art. That precisely this kind of solution was bound up more than any other with contemporary taste, with the historically conditioned ideal of a then still intact bourgeois society, in no way detracts from Bode's great creative achievement.

The ground floor contained for the most part sculptures and reliefs; some rooms also included paintings, where the historical context called for a general display, as in the case of German medieval art. The first floor was given over almost entirely to the Picture Gallery. Here Bode tried to achieve a special ambience by introducing original door-frames, pieces of furniture and works of craftsmanship which were in keeping with the origins of the pictures and heightened their effect. This applied particularly to Italian art, which was displayed in the 'cabinets' and adjoining rooms on the east side, while the development of Netherlandish and German painting could be followed in the suites of rooms on the west side.

A corner of one of the rooms in the Kaiser Friedrich Museum

In the heart of this spacious building, which embraces no less than five inner courtyards, was a large hall, rising through two storeys to a height of more than fifty feet; this, by way of contrast with the didactic nature of the exhibition rooms, embodied Bode's ideal conception of a specific period setting – the so-called Basilica. Although its architectural function was to link the front and rear staircases, and despite the incongruous effect created by its serving as both apse and thoroughfare, it was modelled on the Tuscan church style of *c.* 1500. In the wall-niches were placed altar decorations, faience reliefs by the Robbias and paintings by Vivarini, Francia, Fra Bartolommeo and Paris Bordone; a tomb, two Venetian fountains flanking the entrance, and a choir-stall also helped to recreate a Renaissance atmosphere. The extent to which Bode's very special style of exhibiting works of art was in keeping with contemporary taste, a style which made the Kaiser-Friedrich Museum famous and which can still be seen in various affiliated institutions, emerges clearly from a memorandum written by the Crown Princess, later to become the Empress Victoria. She took an active interest in museum affairs and in a memorandum of 1883 – with the plans for new buildings in mind – recorded her view that exhibition rooms were frequently 'not unlike hospital wards', and therefore 'diminished beyond recognition' the impact of works of art removed from their original surroundings. 'And yet can any nation's architecture perform a finer and more congenial function than to display as effectively as possible the splendid works of art of past ages?'

When the Kaiser-Friedrich Museum was opened, there was also no lack of criticism. But it was directed mainly at architectural shortcomings rather than the impressive display of pictures acquired by Bode which were all here on show for the first time. On the other hand, the architect could not be denied the credit for having solved in an original and artistic way what had seemed an intractable problem. It was really Bode's personal museum style that raised doubts in certain quarters whether he had not allowed the Beelzebub of artistic caprice to drive out the devil of museological moderation. In any case the exhibitions of the Secession, in which the anti-academic painters had banded together, were already showing signs of developing a different style; this trend was shown in a marked preference for an entirely neutral display of each individual work, and very soon began to influence museum practice.

Bode's historical approach led him inevitably to consider anew how best to frame his pictures. Schinkel had designed standard frames for use in the Berlin Gallery and had developed a system of his own for the décor, which divided up pictures into various categories according to their relative importance and identified them accordingly, rather like awarding them badges of rank. Apart from the obvious drawback that relative standards changed with the years and assessments of a past era no longer applied, there was also the element of uniformity, of dull pedagogic dogmatism, that was now felt to have a deadening effect on the appreciation of any particular work of art.

Bode's major achievement was that he recognized the importance of choosing a historically 'relevant' frame if a picture was to be shown to the best advantage, and he demonstrated in the Berlin collection the close aesthetic relationship between frame and picture. He discussed the development of the picture-frame in several contributions to art magazines and was the first to recognize its artistic significance. In adopting a deliberate policy of acquiring original frames for the Picture Gallery, Bode initiated a practice which has persisted to this day, and in fact, despite the severe losses suffered during the Second World War, Berlin still appears to have a finer collection of historical frames than most other museums.

With the opening of the Kaiser-Friedrich Museum, many pictures, which for lack of space had had a very poor showing or had not even been exhibited at all, were put on public display for the first time. As a result a number of gifts were made to the museum, the most noteworthy being that by the Berlin merchant James Simon. Simon, who had successfully expanded the cotton business he inherited from his father, first made the acquaintance of Wilhelm Bode and his closest collaborator Max J. Friedländer when he began buying pictures. With the help of the experts in the museum he built up a private collection, which comprised mainly sculptures and paintings from the Italian Renaissance but also included medieval works. With the presentation of his collection in 1904, which was followed by a second after the First World War, the Picture Gallery acquired an early work by Mantegna, *The Virgin with Sleeping Child*, which is full of lyrical tenderness; besides this – undoubtedly the most important picture in the James Simon Collection – were included a tondo by Raffaelino del Garbo, portraits by Giovanni Bellini, Catena and Bronzino, and panels by Gerard David and Barthel Bruyn.

The inauguration of the new building undoubtedly helped to stimulate the collecting both of pictures and old art in general; in consequence Berlin soon became a centre of international art-dealing. Among the citizens there was a new incentive to make endowments or bequests and government channels became more amenable to making substantial funds available for the purchase of works of art. In 1896 Bode had founded the Kaiser-Friedrich Museum Society, in which more well-to-do citizens pooled their resources in order to purchase – quite independently of State funds – works for the Picture Gallery and the sculpture collection. One of the society's first purchases was Rembrandt's *Man in a Golden Helmet*, one of the best-known pictures in the present collection.

A major addition to the Dutch department came with the purchase around the turn of the century of seven works from the Lord Francis Pelham-Clinton-Hope Collection. These included Vermeer's *Lady and Gentleman drinking Wine*, Jan Steen's *The Christening* and Adriaen van de Velde's famous picture *The Farm*. The original intention to buy two of Gabriel Metsu's finest paintings, *The Letter-writer* and the *Woman reading a Letter*, came to nothing because Bode decided that his budget was already heavily committed, and these works passed to the Alfred Beit collection. Bode hoped that they might eventually come to the gallery by way of a bequest from the collector but this hope was not to be fulfilled.

61

Further important Dutch works came to Berlin in 1907 from the Paris collection of Rudolf Kann, including Rembrandt's *Christ and the Samaritan Woman at the Well* and the study for a *Head of Christ*, as well as paintings by Aert van der Neer, Jacob van Ruisdael and Philips Wouwerman.

Compared with the abundance of minor Dutch masters, the Flemish painters were poorly represented. Even their greatest masters, Rubens and Van Dyck, had only a few, though outstanding works in the gallery. With the completion of the Kaiser-Friedrich Museum and its new skylit rooms, renewed efforts were made to fill the gaps. Two Rubens landscapes from the Lord Francis Pelham-Clinton-Hope Collection, an early work, *The Shipwreck of Aeneas*, and a later picture of Steen Castle, widened the range of subjects covered by this versatile painter. Two more pictures by Rubens were acquired in 1903, the monumental *Conversion of Saint Paul* and the *Portrait of Isabella Brant* (the artist's first wife). Finally two of his later works were obtained from the royal collection, *Diana Bathing* (part of the Orange bequest) and the *Penitent Magdalene*. In 1901 a pair of impressive portraits by Van Dyck, dating from his Genoese period, was purchased from Sir Robert Peel.

The decade that followed the opening of the museum was one of the most successful, but it also marked the end of a glorious period in its history. In order to provide an even more comprehensive coverage of European painting, purchases of works outside the classical field were now made. After the turn of the century the collection of eighteenth-century Italian painting, which had been started in 1878 with the purchase of one of Tiepolo's major works, *The Martyrdom of Saint Agatha*, was systematically expanded. The growing interest in the Venetian painting of the Settecento led to the acquisition of several works by Tiepolo, including the mythological frescoes from the Villa Panigai in Nervesa and several *vedute* by Canaletto and Guardi. The latter's *Balloon Ascent* has since achieved a certain fame.

It was even then too late to acquire major works by Spanish or English painters, particularly as these countries had in any case allowed few native works of art to go abroad. In 1887 Velazquez' *Portrait of Countess Olivares* was purchased, followed in 1906 by one of the same artist's earlier works, *The Three Musicians*, both from English collections. The portrait of the Italian General Alessandro del Borro, purchased in 1873 and at that time attributed to the Spanish master, is today regarded as the work of Andrea Sacchi.

It was not until the beginning of the present century that the gallery succeeded in obtaining pictures by English masters. Apart from two landscapes by Richard Wilson, they were mostly portraits, such as Gainsborough's portrait of John Wilkinson, four works by Reynolds, two each by Romney and Zoffany, and one each by Raeburn and Wilkie, the last of them a sketch for *The Blind Fiddler* in the Tate Gallery, London.

Top-ranking experts paving the way for the expansion and development of the collections on the Museum Island included – in the case of the Picture Gallery – Max J. Friedländer, who had entered the museum service in 1896. His reserved and rather introspective nature was in striking contrast with Bode's restless energy, yet they formed an ideal combination in the field of artistic research. Friedländer was always overshadowed by the older man who, by virtue of the active life he led, gained the credit for the major acquisitions, and Friedländer himself felt that Bode, who was suspicious of any signs of independence in his colleagues, appreciated his weaknesses more than his strength. Bode, for his part, was not unaware of this contrast and recognized the younger man's outstanding talents. 'In a nature striving so hard for efficiency, for tangible results,' Friedländer wrote later of Bode, 'that most powerful motivating force in research, a disinterested love of truth', could not function productively, and it was precisely this latter quality that he possessed and placed, for much of his life, at the service of the Picture Gallery.

Friedländer had an encyclopædic knowledge of early German and particularly Netherlandish painting; between 1924 and 1937 he wrote his fourteen-volume *Die altniederländische Malerei*, which is still a definitive work, and his knowledge undoubtedly contributed to the high standard of the pictures acquired before the First World War. Outstanding among the German paintings are Konrad Witz's small *Christ on the Cross* (1908), Schongauer's *Nativity* (1902), Baldung's late *Lamentation* (1907), and *The Rest on the Flight into Egypt* (1902) by Lucas Cranach the Elder.

A number of major works by the Flemish Primitives were acquired, and fundamentally altered the character of the collection as a whole: van der Weyden's *Portrait of a Young Lady with Coif* (1908); *Christ in the House of Simon* by Dirk Bouts (1904); Geertgen's *Saint John the Baptist* (1902); *Saint John on Patmos* by Hieronymus Bosch (1907); and Pieter Bruegel's *Netherlandish Proverbs*. Most of these pictures, including the German ones, were obtained from English art-dealers or private owners. On the other hand, three important examples of early French painting came from old German collections: Jean Fouquet's panel *Estienne Chevalier with Saint Stephen*, part of a monumental diptych (the other half of which is in the Antwerp Museum), was in the possession of the Brentano family in Frankfurt-on-Main until 1896; the two wings of the St Omer Altarpiece, painted by Simon Marmion in 1459, were acquired from Prince zu Wied in 1905.

The finest additions to the Netherlandish collection were acquired in Spain: Hugo van der Goes' *The Adoration of the Shepherds* (the property of Maria Cristina of Bourbon) from Madrid in 1903, and the altarpiece with *The Adoration of the Magi* from the Monforte monastery in 1913. In 1897 Bode had tried to obtain for Berlin one of van der Goes' major works, the

Portinari Altarpiece (now in the Uffizi Gallery), which was put up for sale by the Hospital of S. Maria Nuova in Florence, but the Italian government intervened. The purchase of the Monforte Altarpiece also threatened to fall through at the last moment. The picture had been auctioned in May 1911 and knocked down to the Berlin bidder for around 950,000 gold marks, but there followed a change of Cabinet in the Spanish government, which had previously agreed to the sale, and a ban was placed on the export of the altarpiece. After a tug-of-war lasting two and a half years Madrid finally lifted the ban. In December 1913 Friedländer supervised the transport of the heavy panels (the wings are lost) from Monforte to Berlin, where they were exhibited in the museum on the first day of Christmas and – in Bode's own words – 'evoked universal admiration'.

A few months later the fateful shots were fired at Sarajevo. For several years the world was embroiled in a war which among other things dealt a death-blow to the German Empire. The days of easy money were over and with them passed the splendour of the Bode era. In fact, the Monforte Altarpiece was the last truly great acquisition by the Berlin Picture Gallery, for no single purchase made in the half-century since then can compare with it.

THE GERMAN MUSEUM

The Kaiser-Friedrich Museum suffered the same fate as many other newly built museums, in that it had no sooner been completed than it lacked space. This was not so much a consequence of the rapid growth of the Picture Gallery as of a change in the overall conception, following the establishment of entirely new collections, amongst them the Islamic and Near Eastern department. In particular, the monumental façade of the Palace of Mushatta, which Bode had acquired in Syria in 1903, had to be accommodated provisionally on the ground floor of the Kaiser-Friedrich Museum as there was no room elsewhere for this 150-ft wide architectural exhibit. In addition the original idea of a Renaissance Museum had been considerably watered down, if not abandoned altogether, during the years when the museum was being planned and built. It had been said of Bode that he was a typical child of his time in that he introduced into the museum world the 'renaissancist' movement represented by Friedrich Nietzsche, Jacob Burckhardt and Conrad Ferdinand Meyer. But Bode was too much of a realist to ignore the changing conditions of his time and to subordinate them to a personal ideal.

In February 1907 Bode issued a memorandum, in which he called for the construction of still further museum buildings to relieve the pressure on the existing collections and to enable new collections to develop unhindered. In a forward-looking survey he outlined his plan for a museum-complex on the Spree island. To include as an integral part of this a new museum for early German art seemed to him a duty 'on national grounds alone' as well as a necessity for the national capital as no museum of this kind existed in the whole of Germany. 'It will, by recognizing those qualities that are peculiarly German, help to refine and promote our modern art, to stimulate and ennoble it.'

In formulating these ideas Bode was still motivated by the old ambition to establish a Renaissance Museum, for in the German Museum which he was planning he wanted to include not only German art but the entire range of medieval art of the Nordic countries, and to remove these from the Kaiser-Friedrich Museum. The architectonic planning, which presented very serious problems in the limited space still available on the Museum Island, was

65

entrusted to Alfred Messel, who was appointed museum architect in 1907. He solved the problem brilliantly and produced designs which harmonized with the existing buildings by Schinkel, Stüler, Strack and Ihne. A large building, consisting of three wings and a ceremonial court facing west, would accommodate three branches of culture: late antiquity, Oriental art and German art. The Pergamon Museum, with the famous altar in the centre, formed the nucleus of the complex, the south wing of which was to be devoted to the Near Eastern Museum, the north wing to the German Museum.

From the moment work on this vast building started in 1909, it was dogged by misfortune. In the very first year its designer, Alfred Messel, died and his friend and pupil, Ludwig Hoffmann, had to take over. The condition of the site was such that it was necessary to lay special foundations, the cost of which far exceeded the original estimates. Finally, with the outbreak of the First World War, work came to a complete standstill. The economic situation following the military defeat and the Treaty of Versailles made the resumption of work impossible, and furthermore Bode's whole conception was now felt to be outdated and was the subject of violent criticism by the Press.

After Messel's original design had been trimmed down considerably, the building was finally completed in 1930. The German Museum in the north wing, which was linked with the Kaiser-Friedrich Museum by a footbridge over the railway, was exactly as Bode had conceived and planned it. Instead of 'the traditional museological barriers' there was to be a close association of sculpture, painting and applied art, which would engender a better understanding of the culture of any given period and region.

The ground floor was to house medieval art of the thirteenth and fourteenth centuries. Full justice was done to the astonishing wealth of panel-paintings from this period by displaying them in the chapel-like window-niches of a large hall. The rooms on the first floor began with examples of the nascent realism that characterized the mid-fifteenth century, the great panels of the Wurzach Altar by Hans Multscher occupying a prominent place, and continued on to the German painters of the seventeenth and eighteenth centuries. In the small, adjoining rooms, the great masters of the Renaissance – Dürer, Baldung, Altdorfer and Holbein – were shown, and likewise the precious collection of early Netherlandish pictures. Friedländer, who succeeded Bode in 1929, realized that the term 'German', even if employed 'in as wide a sense as possible and racially rather than geographically or politically', did not always adequately describe the works on display.

Bode, whose last years had been devoted largely to the German Museum, did not live to see it completed. He died on 1 March 1929 at the age of 84, after more than fifty years in the museum service. His death marked the end of an era which had lost something of its brilliance since the collapse of the

German Empire but still exercized a peculiar fascination. All the emotionalism and sentimentality of the Wilhelmine period surged up again as Bode's last remains lay in princely state in the Basilica of the Kaiser-Friedrich Museum; here he had earlier realized his conception of an ideal Renaissance interior and integrated it with the cultural life of the museum.

The outcome of the First World War can have left no doubts in anyone's mind that the period of expansion was also over for the State museums. Bode's museum policy had been much too closely linked with the image of the German Empire for the future of the art collections not to be in jeopardy. The acute economic crisis and the urgent need to complete the new buildings, which had stood for years unfinished, left very little scope for new acquisitions, and indeed some depletion of the collection had to be accepted. For the first time in the history of the Picture Gallery the total number of works of art, which for almost a hundred years had grown progressively, was appreciably reduced by foreign intervention. Now, in accordance with Article 247 of the Treaty of Versailles, Van Eyck's Ghent Altarpiece, which had been in Berlin since 1818 as part of the Solly Collection, had to be handed over to the Belgian State in 1920, together with the wings of the Louvain Altar by Dirk Bouts, which Waagen had acquired in 1834.

It is easy enough to condemn, on grounds of principle or international law, such levies imposed by the victors, but few would be prepared to dispute the great benefit – in the artistic sense – that resulted from the return of the altar-wings to their place of origin after an absence of several centuries; admittedly these were major sacrifices but ones which could hardly be questioned, considering the appalling devastation that had been inflicted on Belgium's art-treasures.

Compared with the dynamic development during the pre-war period, the financial resources of the Picture Gallery between the wars were very modest, yet ways and means were still found to acquire several important works. In 1924 the Rembrandt *Landscape with a Bridge* was purchased from the Duke of Oldenburg; the full range of this highly versatile artist was now represented in Berlin. The Rubens collection also gained two outstanding landscapes, both of distinguished provenance: one, acquired in 1928, was in small format, and had originally been in the collection of Charles I of England; the other – acquired in 1927, and of massive proportions – had been in the collection of the Duc de Richelieu. Friedländer acquired (1931) a second work by Pieter Bruegel the Elder, *Two Chained Monkeys*, to augment the Netherlandish paintings. New acquisitions among the French painters were Georges de la Tour's *Saint Sebastian* (1928) and Chardin's *The Draughtsman* (1931). Elsheimer's *Holy Family* was purchased (1928) for the German department.

THE SECOND WORLD WAR
AND THE FRIEDRICHSHAIN
DISASTER

From the time of its accession to power in 1933 the Hitler regime caused serious disruption in the Berlin museums. Many art-connoisseurs were removed from office, discriminated against or even forced to emigrate. Max Friedländer, at the age of 67, was one of those compelled to leave his native city for ever. International art-dealers, who, encouraged by Bode's activities, had made Berlin one of their leading auction-centres, withdrew from Germany altogether. The large private collections in Berlin, which Bode had helped to build up, were dispersed or found their way abroad. The government decreed that the James Simon Collection must no longer be exhibited separately under the name of that great patron of Prussia's museums, and that its individual works must be incorporated in the appropriate departments. Fortunately the magnanimous founder of this collection was spared the indignity of seeing his wishes so flagrantly disregarded. Hitler's autarchic ambitions and his preparations for war led to severe currency restrictions, which made the international art-market inaccessible to the German museums. The few acquisitions that were made during this period for the Picture Gallery bear the inevitable blemish of the barter-deal, which – as museum-history has shown – is hardly ever favourable to the initiator.

At the outbreak of war, on 1 September 1939, the museums in Berlin – as in other European capitals – were closed so as to enable suitable steps to be taken for the protection of their contents against possible air-attack. It was not the first time that the Museum Island had experienced such a situation; in the spring of 1938, when Hitler invaded Czechoslovakia, the government had ordered the temporary evacuation of the building and the removal of the pictures to air-raid shelters, though whether from genuine concern for their safety or simply for propaganda purposes is by no means clear. At least the experience proved useful when the pictures had to be moved again in autumn 1939, for the time being to the basement vaults of the museum where their conservation could be properly supervised, but as the air-attacks increased in 1942–43 the vaults seemed less and less secure. In the meantime, bomb-proof bunkers had been built in the Berlin area with anti-aircraft guns on their roofs; with their lifts and ventilation-plants, these shelters were also suitable for storing works of art. At the same time, space was limited, so that only the best works from the various departments of the museum could be accommodated. The Picture Gallery was allotted rooms in the Friedrichshain bunker which proved to be climatically sound, and it was even possible to keep the more delicate works under constant supervision.

In 1943 the air-raids on Berlin by British aircraft had, between March and the end of the year, inflicted severe damage on the Museum Island and particularly on the New Museum. In the months that followed, further damage was done by bomb-blast to skylights, windows and doors; finally, in a daylight raid on 3 February 1945, American bombers scored twenty-five direct hits on the Museum Island alone. All the buildings suffered severely and two months later, when the Allied ground forces converged on Berlin, still more damage was done by artillery bombardment.

The bunkers had until then proved thoroughly effective as shelters for the art-treasures, as they withstood even the most violent attacks. But the news that Berlin was to be defended against the advancing Allied armies created a completely new situation. In March 1945 urgent steps were taken to evacuate all the works of art from the threatened capital, and previous objections to the use of disused salt-mines for their storage now had to be abandoned. The museum's treasures were transported some 200 miles by lorry to mines at Ransbach and Kaiseroda-Merkers, south of Eisenach. The first convoy left the capital on 13 March, six weeks before the city surrendered, and within a few days 1,225 pictures had been transported. At the end of March the Allied armies encircling Berlin began to close in, so that further evacuation became impossible. Important works had to remain in the bunkers, partly because the cases containing them were too large to be lowered down the mine-shafts.

The capture and occupation of Berlin, which the Western Allies had left to the Red Army, was completed in the last days of April and the final surrender of the city followed on 2 May. Soviet soldiers took over the bunkers with their priceless contents intact and ejected the museum-watchmen on duty there. A few days later occurred the disaster which has acquired a tragic notoriety and which will always be associated with the name of Friedrichshain. In circumstances which have never been explained fire broke out in both storeys of the bunker, destroying all the works of art which were stored there. The hope that this or that work might – for whatever reason – have survived the holocaust has not been abandoned to this day, as the responsible occupying power refused to allow an investigation and has so far failed to make any official statement. Berlin museum-officials were not called in when the Russians searched the debris.

The destruction of more than 400 pictures, not a few of them masterpieces in their own right, and of an equally large number of no less important sculptures is the most serious loss that any single art-collection has ever suffered. However, such was the appalling toll of human victims in 1945 that it took a considerable time for the public to become aware of the extent of this disaster.

The large paintings by the Flemish and Italian masters, which had been an outstanding feature of the Berlin collection, were the hardest hit. The loss of Signorelli's *Pan, God of Nature*, a quite unique work of its kind, was irretrievable, as was that of the monumental Renaissance altarpieces by Fra Bartolommeo, Francia, Moretto, Sarto, Roberti and Vivarini, to mention only a few; the outstanding Baroque works from the Giustiniani Collection, including three pictures by Caravaggio and Guido Reni's *Saints Paul and Anthony*, were also destroyed. Among the Flemish masters eight works by Rubens alone were lost, including *The Conversion of Saint Paul*, *Neptune and Amphitrite* and *Diana Bathing*, as were four Van Dyck paintings, including the *Bacchanale*, and all the Jordaens pictures. The Spanish section, which was in any case small, was deprived of two of its most important works, Murillo's *Saint Anthony* and Zurbarán's *Saint Bonaventure*; where French pictures were concerned, Vouet's *Annunciation* and Lebrun's portrait of Everhard Jabach and his family were the most serious losses. On the other hand – thanks to the fact that most of them were of smaller format and had been evacuated from the bunker – the early German paintings and the Dutch Baroque masters suffered less severely, but even here the destruction of the huge Quedlinburg Retable, dating from *c.* 1250, was a bitter blow. Other important works of the Dutch school – by Thomas de Keyser, Nicolaes Maes, Gerard Terborch, Emanuel de Witter and Nicolaes Berchem – were also consumed by the flames.

In retrospect, one can only regard it as a near-miracle that most of the paintings were rescued at the last moment, before the city was finally cut off; a few weeks earlier, the fire in the Friedrichshain bunker would have effectively destroyed the Berlin Gallery. After hostilities had ceased the pictures stored in Thüringia were removed from the mine by the U.S. Army and transported to Wiesbaden. Here the Landesmuseum, which had only been partially damaged, became the Central Art Collecting Point for the American Occupation Zone. In November 1945 the American authorities selected 202 of the Berlin paintings and sent them to Washington, where they were deposited in the National Gallery. The reason given for this action was the unstable conditions in Germany. Soon after the surrender the Red Army likewise began – on a much bigger scale, to be sure – transporting to the U.S.S.R. works of art found in their zone. Among them were more pictures from the Berlin Gallery which had been stored in the cellars of the museum.

In February 1946, when the war-damage to the Wiesbaden Museum had been repaired, a selection of works from the Berlin Museum, including eighty-nine paintings from the Picture Gallery, were given their first post-war display. This exhibition, which was organized by the American military government in collaboration with German officials, was followed by a number of others. The tenth of these, in the summer of 1949, was a special occasion for it marked an event to gladden the hearts of all German, and particularly Berlin, art-connoisseurs: the return of the 202 paintings from Washington.

The President of the United States had already agreed to their return in February 1948, but, as they had not been shown in public, it was decided to exhibit them in Washington before shipping them back to Germany. Shortly afterwards Congress adopted a resolution to send the pictures – with the exception of fifty-two which were not in a fit state to travel – on a tour of the United States, involving twelve other American cities. Although the most careful preparations were made, with the collaboration of German experts, and the most elaborate security precautions taken, the paintings were exposed to considerable physical hazards: within a period of twelve months they were exhibited in thirteen cities, which meant, on each occasion, being packed and unpacked, loaded and unloaded, and altogether being transported over 12,000 miles in every kind of climate. It is therefore not surprising that successively, in almost every city, a number of pictures had to be removed at the first sign of deterioration in their condition.

The exhibition received an unusual amount of publicity, which included some quite inaccurate descriptions and reports of the origin of the pictures. It was claimed, for example, that these works had been looted by Hitler in occupied Europe and had been discovered by American troops in secret hiding-places. In not a few of the cities the transporting of the paintings from the railway-station to the exhibition-hall was turned into a parade complete with military band and tanks. Almost 2,500,000 people visited these exhibitions, which finally ended in Toledo, Ohio, in March 1949. The net profit of over 300,000 dollars was handed over to the American occupation authorities to help German children in the American zone.

At the end of April the military transport vessel *General Patch* left New York harbour with its priceless cargo and sailed for Germany. Conditions had by now become sufficiently stable for the Western Powers to transfer responsibility for internal administration to the Federal Republic. Accordingly, in 1949 the Berlin art-treasures, which had been delivered to the Wiesbaden Collecting Point, were handed over to the *Land* government of Hesse.

THE PICTURE GALLERY IN THE DAHLEM MUSEUM

Almost ten years had passed since the art-treasures had left the Kaiser-Friedrich Museum. The buildings on the Museum Island – most of them either destroyed or temporarily reinstated – now lay in the Eastern sector of the divided city. The victors of 1945 had become hopelessly bogged down in disputes over the ruins of Hitler's Third Reich, and Berlin was the focal point of an international political conflict which was assuming alarming proportions. This reached its climax in June 1948, when the Soviet Union imposed the blockade which made it necessary for the Allied powers to organize an airlift for eleven months to keep the Western sectors of Berlin supplied. But if this situation in itself offered little if any prospect of an early rehabilitation of the Berlin collection, the drastic changes made by the victors in the traditional political structure of the German Reich were to have even more far-reaching consequences. On 25 February 1947 the Allied Control Council decreed in Law No. 46 that Prussia should cease to exist as a separate state. This decision, for which there is no precedent in modern times, ran contrary to all the logic of history; for the Berlin museums it meant no more and no less than the abolition of their legal status and indeed of their very existence.

The Federal Republic, established in 1949 and comprising the American, British and French occupation zones, had no powers at that stage to deal with the property of the recently dissolved Prussian State. The Federal government took the view that the best solution would be to transfer the ownership of the Prussian art-treasures in their entirety to the Federal Republic, but this was immediately resisted by the *Land* governments which were not prepared, on constitutional grounds, to allow the Federal government any jurisdiction in cultural affairs; and the fact that a large part of what had once been Prussia now lay outside the boundaries of the Federal Republic strengthened the case for bringing the Prussian art-treasures, which were still on the Western side, together under the control of a properly constituted body. This idea was first put forward in 1950 but many years were to pass before all the conflicting interests could be reconciled and plans modified sufficiently to meet with general approval.

73

Even though it was agreed that a special body should be set up, the cost of which would be met by the *Land* governments, it was found impossible to work out a legal formula which was acceptable to all. Unfortunately it was not merely divergent views over questions of law that held up the negotiations but also blatant self-interest on the part of several *Land* governments. These quarrels, which in the long run could only damage the cause of the Berlin collections, naturally aroused dismay and criticism among the general public. In fact, it was not until 6 May 1955 – ten years after the war had ended – that a provisional agreement was finally reached, in which the *Land* governments of Baden-Württemberg, Berlin, Hesse, Lower Saxony, North Rhine-Westphalia, Rhineland-Palatinate and Schleswig-Holstein accepted a commitment to take joint administrative responsibility for the Prussian art-treasures.

This agreement at long last provided a legal justification for the rehabilitation of the Berlin collections on a broader basis, a task which the Berlin Senate could not solve alone. The division of the city, which had culminated in the Berlin blockade, made it abundantly clear that, for the foreseeable future at least, there could be no prospect of returning the Berlin art-treasures from storage in West Germany to the Museum Island in the Eastern sector. The Senate had therefore decided, as early as 1950, to extend the Museum of Ethnology originally established at Bode's instigation in the western suburb of Dahlem. Construction work, begun in 1912, had been interrupted by the First World War and for over thirty years the unfinished building had been used to house the ethnological collections. The completion and extension of the Dahlem Museum now provided sufficient space to justify the return of the paintings. At a time when Berlin was in a state of permanent political crisis, this was regarded as a striking demonstration that the Senate was seeking to rehabilitate the Prussian collections in West Berlin.

On 2 October 1950 the Oberbürgermeister of Berlin, Ernst Reuter, formally opened the Dahlem Museum with an exhibition of works from the Berlin Museum. A total of 149 paintings from the Picture Gallery, which were flown in from Wiesbaden, returned to Berlin for the first time since the end of the war. This exhibition was followed by several others but on each occasion the trustees appointed by Hesse insisted on the return of the works of art to the Wiesbaden depot. This rigid adherence to legal formalities and lack of confidence in conditions in Berlin meant that repeated transportation by air exposed the art-treasures to intolerable hazards. The Kaiser-Friedrich Museum Society, which Wilhelm Bode had founded in 1897 to support the Picture Gallery, quite rightly took the view that there was no legal justification for a loan-arrangement, at least where the works of art which it owned were concerned. In 1953 the Society was granted a court order for the return of more than fifty paintings, including Rembrandt's *Man in a Golden Helmet*, to the Dahlem Museum, thus paving the way for the subsequent restoration of all the museum's property to Berlin.

By May 1957 all the pictures belonging to the Picture Gallery had been returned from the Wiesbaden depot, and since then, subject only to the exigencies of space, a selection of the finest works has been permanently on display in the Dahlem Museum. Shortly afterwards, on 25 July 1957, the Federal parliament in Bonn passed a law to establish a special foundation to take charge of former Prussian cultural property – the *Stiftung Preussischer Kulturbesitz*. The *Land* governments immediately questioned the validity of this law and the dispute went to the Federal Constitutional Court. In July 1959, after two years of wrangling, the dispute was settled in favour of the Federal government. In practice, however, the newly founded body was able to begin work only in 1961, when the problems of its charter and finances were resolved.

The story of the Federal Republic's cultural policy still remains to be written. It is one of the less impressive chapters in the history of post-war Germany. It took the *Land* governments more than ten years to agree on what should happen to the most important art-collection of the former German *Reich*. The fact that this remarkable national heirloom was, for a long time, deprived of any real legal status and was even threatened with dissolution, that its rehabilitation was impeded and its enormous potential value as an educational and artistic treasure-house was not exploited, aroused justifiable dismay and criticism – particularly outside Germany. Moreover it is hardly an encouraging sign of cultural awareness that, after years of disagreement, only three *Land* governments other than Berlin (North Rhine-Westphalia, Baden-Württemberg and Schleswig-Holstein) have so far seen their way to joining the foundation and helping to ensure the preservation of the Prussian collections.

The establishment of the *Stiftung Preussicher Kulturbesitz* must be regarded as a historic achievement. It provides for the works of art entrusted to it an administrative framework jointly financed, in accordance with the federal principle of the constitution, by the Federal and *Land* governments. It is the declared aim of the *Stiftung* to maintain the Prussian collections in their traditional context, and its charter also provides for the reconstruction and future development of the Berlin museums.

For more than twenty years the Picture Gallery in the Dahlem Museum has been open to the public. As the same building also houses the sculptures, the engravings and the ethnological collections, only a limited number of pictures can be shown. While the visitor of today may welcome this concentration, those who were familiar with the old Kaiser-Friedrich Museum

The façade and main entrance of the Dahlem Museum

cannot fail to notice especially the absence of the large paintings destroyed in the bunker fire in 1945, and the splendid display of pictures by minor masters which the gallery once boasted. Memories of the collection are inevitably dimmed – a collection which had been so systematically built up and of which the pictures still extant on the Museum Island formed a part. Since the return in 1958 of those pictures that were removed to the Soviet Union, there remain some 900 paintings on the Museum Island; of these a small selection is displayed in the former Kaiser-Friedrich Museum which in 1956 was renamed the Bode Museum.

With the transfer of the Picture Gallery to Dahlem it became possible for the building to resume the normal functions of a museum. After years of being moved from place to place, all the pictures were in need of special

76

conservation. The whole work of scientific cataloguing and even of photographic reproduction had to start again from scratch. The partial destruction and dispersal of the original collection had radically changed its complexion, and at the same time the values accorded to individual schools and periods had also undergone a considerable change over the past few decades. This new situation had to be taken into account in acquiring additions to the gallery, and, with the limited means available, the policy has been mainly to make good the wartime losses. The sad fact remains that no adequate substitute for some of the works destroyed can ever be found; on the other hand, several gaps have been filled. A few names should suffice to give some idea of the gallery's acquisitions during the past twenty years. The Flemish and Dutch schools were strengthened with works by Aertsen, Jordaens, Snyders, Terborch, Asselyn, Berchem and Pynacker; acquisitions of French and Italian paintings include works by Garofalo, Bassano, Annibale Carracci, Guercino, Liss, Magnasco, Rosa, Giordano, Le Nain and Vouet. The large gaps in the Spanish and English schools were partially filled by pictures by El Greco and Murillo, and Gainsborough, respectively.

Since the Dahlem building was originally designed as a museum and was never intended to accommodate a picture gallery, it lacks large skylit rooms and the standard of lighting for the display of paintings is generally poor. In view of the enormous damage done to the city during the war, the decision to house the art-treasures in Dahlem could only be regarded as a welcome expedient, which was never envisaged as more than a provisional solution, at least as long as there was still even a remote prospect of ending the division of Berlin and returning to the Museum Island. Even when it became clear that the lot of the State Museums could only be improved by extending the existing buildings, the scope for locating all museum departments permanently in Dahlem was limited by the fact that the Free University, founded in 1948, needed every inch of available building-land in that part of the city. It was not until the *Stiftung Preussischer Kulturbesitz* had placed the administration of the museums on a regular footing that adequate financial resources were made available to enable long-term plans to be made. In 1962 it was decided – in accordance with Wilhelm Bode's original idea – that only the ethnological, Near Eastern and Asiatic collections should be permanently housed in Dahlem. New buildings would be erected in the centre of the city, on the south side of the Tiergarten, to accommodate the Western art-treasures.

In 1968 the first of these new buildings was opened, the New National Gallery designed by Mies van der Rohe and intended for nineteenth- and twentieth-century art. From here to the original buildings on the Museum Island is a mere one-and-a-half miles, a very short distance in a large city, but for practical purposes the way is barred by the Berlin Wall. In the same area, where only a small church from the Schinkel period survived the tank-battles and street-fighting of April 1945, a new Picture Gallery will eventually be built on a site near the New National Gallery and the Philharmonie (concert hall) which was completed in 1963. It is a site that has been chosen with a brighter future in mind, in the hope that one day Berlin will cease to be a divided city and that the road from the Tiergarten to the Museum Island will once again be open to normal traffic.

THE PLATES

BOHEMIAN MASTER, c. 1350
The Virgin enthroned with Child (The Glatz Madonna). Panel, 186 × 95 cm. Cat. No. 1624.

The Mother of God sits on a richly ornate throne with the Child in her lap, a sceptre and imperial orb in her left hand. From a baldachin behind, an angel leans over and places a crown on the Virgin's head. The throne, the lower parts of which imitate Gothic church architecture, has a most unusual shape and looks almost two-dimensional. The naturalistic treatment of the grain of the wood is in striking contrast to the painted architectural portions and to the gilded sections of the picture. On the elaborate surrounding framework seven angels are shown, some busily engaged, others merely looking out of the piers or even sitting in highly precarious positions to display a fine tapestry. The baldachin is flanked on either side by a chapel-like structure housing a lion.

By the steps of the throne the donor, Archbishop Ernst von Pardubic, kneels bareheaded; his mitre, gloves and pastoral staff lie on the ground in front of him. The Archbishop grew up in Glatz, studied in Prague and then spent 14 years in Italy, mainly at the Universities of Padua and Bologna. On his return to Prague he was appointed first dean, then bishop. He travelled to the papal court at Avignon to be confirmed in this office and in 1344 succeeded in having the see of Prague elevated to an archbishopric. His high office gave him considerable powers of patronage and also, as adviser to Charles IV, a far-reaching influence in political matters. He donated this picture to the Augustinian collegiate foundation at Glatz, in Silesia, which he himself had founded in 1350 and which in 1597 passed to the Jesuits. Some twenty years later, during the Thirty Years' War, they were compelled to flee, but the altar-panel had, it seems, already been removed to a place of safety. At all events, when the Jesuits returned, they brought it back and placed it in the Franciscan College at Glatz, its location when a chronicler described it in 1664; it was later moved to the adjacent school, from which the Berlin Gallery acquired it in 1902.

The rich historico-biographical background, together with the artistic importance of the work have ensured for it a special position in the history of European painting. It appears to be the centre panel of a multipartite altarpiece. A life-history of the bishop, which appeared in 1664, refers also to the Birth of Christ, the Circumcision, the Flight into Egypt, and the Presentation of Christ in the Temple, being represented in smaller format.

The flatness of the bodies and the darkness of the flesh-colours are reminiscent of Byzantine icon painting, while the elegant and imaginative movement of the folds in the dress is a product of French cathedral sculpture and book-illustration. Apart from the donor's close relationship with Italy, which was perhaps also important for the unknown painter, the papal court at Avignon was the link between the Trecento art of Italy and the north.

KONRAD WITZ, before 1410–1444/46
Christ on the Cross. Panel, 34 × 26 cm. Cat. No. 1656.

The Cross stands in an undulating landscape. The scene is profoundly peaceful, giving no suggestion of the place of execution as recorded in the Bible; the two thieves and the soldiers are missing. Only the mourners stand under the Cross, the Virgin on the left, supported by two female companions, and Saint John on the right, wringing his hands in anguish; yet, far from conveying a deep sense of emotion, they seem almost like travellers who have stopped to pray by a wayside cross. The donor of the picture is shown kneeling beside the stony path, his hands raised in prayer, his eyes turned heavenwards.

Almost the entire width of the background is taken up by a lake; a town and a fortified castle stand on its rocky shore. They are depicted with such precision as to suggest a definite locality, but the topographical details have never been identified with any known place. However, Lake Geneva suggests itself as one possibility, since the painter spent the greater part of his life in the Swiss countryside.

The motif of the Cross in an open landscape was one with which Witz would have become acquainted through the Netherlandish painters. The nature of the composition, the attitude of the kneeling donor, the mourners in their loose, flowing robes, the landscape and, not least, the fleecy clouds in the sky recall Van Eyck and Rogier van der Weyden. On the other hand, there is nothing in the artist's little-documented life-history to indicate how he came to be influenced by them. Witz was born at Rottweil in Swabia, probably in the first decade of the fifteenth century. From 1434 onwards he lived in Basle, where he painted the so-called Altar of the Redemption, the several panels of which have found their way into different collections. One, representing the Queen of Sheba before Solomon (p. 262), is in the Berlin Gallery. In Geneva he completed the altar for St Peter's Cathedral in 1444, but thereafter he disappears into obscurity, and in 1447 his wife was registered as a widow. Both the altarpieces show a highly individual and unmistakable style but give no real hint as to Konrad Witz's artistic antecendents. The Berlin *Crucifixion* is of special interest, in that it was clearly painted in the earlier period of the artist's life, before he settled in Basle. In it one can see the first manifestation of the new realism, which, in the second quarter of the century, begins to replace the courtly, elegant, so-called 'soft' style.

Nothing is known of the early history of this picture. It was purchased from a private owner in London in 1908.

HANS MULTSCHER, c. 1400–c. 1467
The Resurrection. Panel, 148 × 140 cm. Cat. No. 1621G.
Signed and dated 1437

The Risen Christ, draped only in a bright red cloth, sits on a massive stone sarcophagus, the red seals on the lid of which are unbroken. The body of Christ bears the stigmata of the Crucifixion. His right hand is raised in the gesture of benediction, while in the left He holds a staff surmounted by a cross. In the confined space between the sarcophagus and the enclosing fence four armed soldiers lie in a deep sleep.

The *Resurrection* is one of the panels from a winged altar of considerable dimensions which has been lost without trace. Originally there was a carved central shrine, in which a Crucifixion group was probably represented. When the wings were closed, the altar showed four scenes relating to the Madonna; these (from top left to bottom right) were *The Nativity, The Adoration of the Magi, The Descent of the Holy Ghost* and *The Death of the Virgin.* When opened, the inner sides of the wings showed four scenes from the Passion, which flanked the central *Crucifixion.* Thus *Christ on the Mount of Olives* (top left), served as a companion-piece to *Christ before Pilate* (top right), while *Christ bearing the Cross* (bottom left), was placed opposite *The Resurrection.*

The original location of the altar has never been established. When it was dismantled, the front and rear sides of the wings became separated. On the two lower panels of the closed altar, showing *The Descent of the Holy Ghost* and *The Death of the Virgin,* the artist appended his signature: 'bitte got für hanssen muoltscheren vo richehove burg ze ulm haut dz werk gemacht do ma zalt MCCCCXXXVII'. Records show that in 1427 the Swabian artist, who came from Reichenhafen near Leutkirch, became a burgher of Ulm, where he worked not only as a painter but more often as a sculptor and engraver. The strength and solidity of the painted figures and their remarkable realism leave one in no doubt that Multscher combined the skills of both sculptor and painter, even though, in keeping with medieval practice, he may well have made use of a well-staffed workshop.

This panel – together with seven others, all of which once formed part of the dismantled altar – was formerly in the gallery of Count Truchsess von Waldburg in Wurzach Castle. All these panels from the so-called 'Wurzach Altar' were taken to England and sold some time before 1803. In 1900 Sir Julius Wernher in London presented them to the Berlin Gallery.

MARTIN SCHONGAUER, c. 1445–1491
The Nativity. Panel, 37·5 × 28 cm. Cat. No. 1629.

In the porch of a house the Virgin kneels beside the Child lying before her on a tattered blanket spread over a bundle of straw. Shepherds approach from the right to worship the Child. Between the wooden posts supporting the roof of the stable we have a glimpse of a hilly landscape with a river flowing through it.

In Schongauer's paintings, as in Dürer's, draughtsmanship is all important. This is well exemplified by the small Berlin panel, which may once have formed part of a small altar and which, for fine detail, could hardly be surpassed. It was natural, therefore, that as early as the sixteenth century, Rogier van der Weyden should have been regarded as Schongauer's teacher. Although this is most unlikely, as Rogier died in 1464, it is nevertheless relevant to the Netherlandish training which Schongauer received. About 1469/70 he visited both Burgundy and the Netherlands, where as his early works show, he made a particularly close study of the works of Rogier, including the Bladelin Altar (p. 115), which was then in Middelburg and is now in Berlin.

Martin Schongauer was the most important German painter and copper-engraver before Dürer. In the latter capacity in particular, he won a reputation that extended beyond the frontiers of Germany. The young Dürer was one of his admirers and was anxious to meet him, but their paths never crossed. Schongauer, who came from Colmar in Alsace, was, like Dürer, the son of a goldsmith, and the skills they inherited undoubtedly contributed to the fact that both artists became masters in the art of copper-engraving.

In 1471, Schongauer settled in his native town, Colmar. It was here, in 1473, that he produced his major painting, the *Madonna of the Rosehedge*, for St Martin's Church in Colmar. The small Berlin panel must have been painted fairly soon after and may have helped to earn him the affectionate nickname, which his own contemporaries converted into a proper name: Martin Schön or Hübsch Martin.

Of the early history of this picture, which was acquired for the Berlin Gallery from a London art-dealer in 1902, nothing is known.

ALBRECHT DÜRER, 1471–1528
The Madonna of the Siskin. Panel, 91 × 76 cm. Cat. No. 557F.
Signed and dated 1506

The Virgin, depicted here with flowing, fair hair, is seated before a red backcloth in a landscape, while two angels hold a garland of roses over her head. The Child is shown playing with a siskin and holding a sugar-castor in his right hand. The Madonna's left hand rests on a book, and with the other she takes a spray of lily of the valley which the young Saint John is holding out to her.

On a wooden bench in the foreground lies a piece of paper bearing the painter's signature in Latin: 'Albertus durer germanus faciebat post virginis partum 1506'. That Dürer should here describe himself specifically as German is not surprising when one takes into account his admiration for the Italian artists. He has included quite a few Venetian touches in this picture and was obviously proud of his achievement. The type of half-length figure he has adopted for the Madonna is modelled on southern paintings and the characteristic blue and red colour-scheme is adopted from Giovanni Bellini, whom Dürer, as he wrote in a letter to Nuremberg at the time, regarded as 'the best of all painters'. The flying cherubim, bodyless angels, were also derived from the Italian Renaissance masters. Saint John, presenting the flowers, is closely akin to the small figure in Titian's *Madonna of the Cherries* in the Vienna Gallery, which was not painted until the second decade of the century. Here the Venetian master showed his respect for the German artist.

Quite a lot is known about Dürer's visit to Venice in 1506. He received a major commission from the German merchants at the Fondaco dei Tedeschi, who later also commissioned works from Giorgione and Titian; Dürer's work, the *Festival of the Rosary*, now in Prague, proved a difficult task which kept him busy and preoccupied for a long time, as he himself admitted; as a result he lost other commissions. He had only the last quarter of the year 1506 in which to complete the *Madonna of the Siskin*, for the following spring he returned to Nuremberg; thus is became an Italian Christmas picture, as the inscription 'after the confinement of the Virgin' expressly states. There are four extant studies for this painting, in which the Child, the cherubim and a piece of drapery are portrayed (Bremen, Paris, Vienna). These sketches also show how closely the creation of the Berlin panel was linked with the *Festival of the Rosary*.

Painted for an unknown patron, the work was probably in the palace of Rudolf II in Prague, that 'great imperial reservoir of Dürer works' (Friedländer), assuming that Carel van Mander's description of 1618 – 'a Madonna, over whom two angels hold a garland of roses, with which to crown her' – refers to this painting. How it came from Italy to Prague is as much a mystery as its subsequent movements. In the 1860s the panel was rediscovered in Scotland; it was in Newbattle Abbey near Edinburgh in 1892 when it was acquired for the Berlin Gallery from the Marquess of Lothian.

ALBRECHT DÜRER, 1471–1528
Portrait of Hieronymus Holzschuher. Panel, 48 × 36 cm. Cat. No. 557E.
Signed AD and dated 1526

Dürer painted this portrait in Nuremberg in 1526, when the sitter was 57 years old. Hieronymus Holzschuher (1469–1529) came from an old Nuremberg patrician family. In 1500 he was elected junior, and nine years later senior burgomaster. In 1514 he ranked as one of the seven Elders of the city government, and on his death in 1529 a commemorative medal bearing his profile was struck. Holzschuher was a fearless champion of the reformation movement in Nuremberg. In Dürer, who was only slightly younger, he found both a sympathizer and a friend. When the painter visited the Netherlands in 1521, he bought presents for Holzschuher, a fact which he noted in his diary.

The artist has filled almost the whole of the upper half of the panel with his subject's powerful head, for which the upper part of the body, clad in heavy fur, seems merely to serve as a plinth, attention being focused on the features. In this portrait Dürer has reproduced details with incredible fidelity. The fine brush has rendered the thick, wavy hair, which has receded somewhat over the forehead, with all the delicacy of a pen-and-ink drawing. At the same time, the face and the full lips are strongly modelled and determine the full-blooded vitality of the man. Reflected in the sitter's eyes are the window-bars of the room in which Dürer worked. Dürer himself fitted to the frame a sliding cover bearing Holzschuher's coat of arms; frame and cover are still extant in their original state and have served for centuries to protect the picture. In 1651 when the painter and art-historian Joachim von Sandrart was commissioned by some distinguished personality, possibly the Elector Maximilian I of Bavaria, to purchase the panel, his offer was turned down on the ground that it was intended to remain in the subject's family as a permanent memorial to him.

During the eighteenth century the picture remained, well looked-after, in a ground-floor room of the family residence. Then, with the growth of romanticism in the early nineteenth century, there was a revival of interest in German painting and this famous portrait was brought out into the light of day. The new-found enthusiasm for Dürer's art made this particular portrait more popular than almost any other work of his. When it was publicly exhibited for the first time in Munich in 1869, it had already been accepted as epitomizing the old German patrician class. The portrait remained in the possession of Holzschuher's descendants in Nuremberg until it was purchased for the Berlin Gallery in 1884.

LUCAS CRANACH THE ELDER, 1472–1553
The Rest on the Flight into Egypt. Panel, 69 × 51 cm. Cat. No. 564 A.
Signed and dated LC 1504

The Virgin has settled down to rest in a meadow on the edge of a forest. Supported by her, the child Jesus reaches out for the strawberries which an angel is offering him. Another angel is drawing water from a spring, a third is bringing a bird, while others sit in the grass and make music. Joseph, holding his hat and staff, stands, as if on guard, behind the group.

The representation of the Holy Family, who have interrupted their journey in a fresh summer landscape, has always been treated as a romantic theme. The poetic overtones of the incident may induce a sense of romanticism in the observer, but the significance of the details should not be overlooked. They are deeply rooted in the traditional symbolism of the Middle Ages. The strawberries, which the angel is offering the Child, were regarded as a divine fruit, and the exotic bird could also be taken as a symbol of paradise. The primrose in the meadow is a Marian symbol, as is the pure water gushing out of the spring. Two other plants, columbine and fumitory, should be noted in connection with the Virgin and Child. Fumitory had a special significance in folk tradition in the choice of bride and bridegroom. The symbolic identification of Jesus with the bridegroom is, of course, already known to us from the Bible (Matthew xxv). Only through an understanding of the symbolic imagery of the period can one appreciate why nature has lost its terrors as a scene of the flight and why the artist turned it into a heavenly garden, which alone seemed appropriate as a resting-place.

What is surprising in Cranach's treatment of landscape is his creation of a magical fairy-tale atmosphere which marked an entirely new approach to nature in European painting. The artist, who was then thirty-two, had embarked upon a revolutionary course, which, in the context of the first five years of the sixteenth century, marks him out as the most advanced of German painters, apart from Dürer. The Berlin panel, the first painting known to bear the artist's signature, is commonly regarded as an early work, but only because we know practically nothing of his activities before 1500.

Cranach, who came from Kronach in Franconia, was from 1505 onwards in the service of the Elector Frederick the Wise of Saxony at his court in Wittenberg. A painting as unusual as *The Rest on the Flight*, which was completed the previous year, may well have helped him to win so notable a position. The period in which the picture was painted coincides with a visit Cranach paid to Austria, of which little is known. He did, however, design a number of woodcuts for book illustrations and painted several portraits, among them, probably, one of the wife of the Viennese scholar Dr Reuss (p. 263) in 1503, now in the Berlin Gallery. *The Rest on the Flight* was clearly inspired by the Danube landscape, and it was this same region which inspired two other German landscape-painters who went much farther along the path Cranach had opened up: Albrecht Altdorfer and Wolf Huber.

In the nineteenth century this picture was in the Sciarra collection in Rome. Bode records in his memoirs his unsuccessful attempt in 1873 to purchase the painting. It passed, instead, into the possession of Dr Conrad Fiedler and finally, in 1902, through his heir, Hermann Levi, to the Berlin Gallery.

92

ALBRECHT ALTDORFER, c. 1480–1538
The Rest on the Flight into Egypt. Panel, 57 × 38 cm. Cat. No. 638 B.
Signed and dated 1510

The Virgin is shown resting in a throne-like chair by a richly ornate Renaissance fountain, while Joseph proffers a basket of cherries. Several angels are playing in and around the basin of the fountain, and the child Jesus tries to reach into the water. The fountain-pillar is lavishly decorated with sculpture. The significance of the group of figures at the top – a bearded man with a boy shooting an arrow – is not clear, but appears to relate to ancient mythology. Beyond the fountain the wooded shores of a lake stretch far into the distance. The rocks are crowded with gateways, fortified roads and towers, houses with pointed gables, ruins and decaying roofs – all so intricately interwoven with trees and foliage that it is difficult to detect the relationship of any one building to another.

The element of fantasy, which so dominates the landscape, is also apparent in the fountain, in which the figures seem to be drawn both from reality and from the artist's imagination. There is no prototype or parallel in Altdorfer's time for the bizarre appearance of the fountain. The painter's artistic invention was in this case at least a generation ahead of his time.

At the foot of the fountain is a stone tablet bearing the Latin inscription: 'Albertus Altdorfer pictor Ratisponensis in salutem animae hoc tibi munus diva maria sacravit corde fideli 1510 AA' ('Albrecht Altdorfer, painter from Regensburg, for the salvation of his soul dedicated this gift to thee, divine Mary, with a faithful heart'); this indicates a very personal confession on the part of the painter, his appeal to the Virgin Mary. The dedication must also be taken as an explanation of the central feature of the picture, the fountain, which – though symbolic of a heathen place – is nonetheless the water of life for the Holy Family. The motif recalls the legend, according to which a spring appeared from the earth when the Holy Family in its flight sought a place to rest. A few years earlier Cranach had treated the same theme (p. 95); this fact establishes a singular bond between the two paintings.

It is assumed that the landscape reproduces impressions from the country near Regensburg, and in particular the hamlets of Scheuchenberg, Lerchenhaube and Wörth, which are also recognizable in Altdorfer's *Crucifixion* in the gallery at Cassel. The painter settled in Regensburg in 1505 and twenty years later was appointed the city's master-builder. Most of his pictures point to a predilection for architecture and architectural décor. An example of this is the highly imaginative construction of the fountain and – on another panel (p. 265) in Berlin painted somewhat later – the ruin in the darkness which serves as the setting for the birth of Christ.

Of the origins of the picture nothing is known. In 1876 it was purchased for the Berlin Gallery from the Friedrich Lippmann collection in Vienna.

ALBRECHT ALTDORFER, c. 1480–1538
Landscape with Satyr Family. Panel, 23 × 20 cm. Cat. No. 638 A.
Signed and dated: AA 1507

A family of satyrs has settled on a tree-covered slope at the foot of a cliff. The man with horns and goat's feet is shown holding a club, while a blonde woman nestles against him and supports the child standing on her thigh. The couple seem to be oblivious of a scene taking place in a nearby meadow, where a woman in a red dress is attempting to flee from a naked man who is carrying a stick in one hand and holding her fast with the other.

The uninhibited way of life of human or semi-human beings in the freedom of natural surroundings was a frequently occurring theme in literary and pictorial works of the Renaissance, following the precedent of antiquity. German artists became familiar with subjects of this kind mainly through copper-engravings by Andrea Mantegna and other northern Italian artists. By no means all these themes were derived straight from antiquity; frequently they were mythological fantasies inspired by Roman relief sculpture.

The whole atmosphere of Altdorfer's idyllic scene suggests that it was inspired not so much by engravings as by the arcadian landscapes of Venetian painters of the school of Giorgione; yet, although the motif of the naked woman seen from behind seems to confirm this, Altdorfer's approach to his art is fundamentally different. The satisfaction of depicting the nude, for which scenes from antiquity provided the most obvious pretext, is entirely subordinate in Altdorfer's paintings to his rendering of nature. The figures, which are fairly summarily treated, remain small and relatively inconspicuous against the dense wooded background. Whether the painter actually visited Venice is not certain but it does seem highly likely. About 1500 he was working in the Salzburg region at the Mondsee monastery, before he acquired burgher's rights in Regensburg in 1505. The present work, produced two years later, is one of Altdorfer's earliest signed and dated paintings. Like Cranach's *Rest on the Flight* (p. 93), painted in 1504, it points the way to a new awareness of landscape in the Renaissance period, originally stemming from the so-called Danube school.

Around the middle of the last century this portrait was in the Kraenner Collection in Regensburg; it later passed into the collection of Barthel Suermondt, which was purchased for the Berlin Gallery in 1874.

HANS BALDUNG GRIEN, 1484/85–1545
The Lamentation of Christ. Panel, 139 × 93 cm. Cat. No. 603 B.

Kneeling beneath the crosses of Calvary, the Virgin mourns her Son whose body lies before her. John supports the dead Christ's head, while Mary Magdalene, her long hair flowing, lifts one of His hands to her cheek. Behind John stands Joseph of Arimathaea with an anointing-vessel, and behind the Virgin rises the upright of the bare cross, stained with the blood of the crucified Saviour; on the tree next to it can be seen the bound foot of one of the thieves. Beyond is a rocky landscape with a castle on the edge of a lake.

Apart from the Berlin panel, the theme of the Lamentation occurs in only one other painting by Baldung. The picture in the Landesmuseum at Innsbruck, which bears the date 1513 and is clearly an earlier work, is much more constricted, more angular and restless in its composition. In the Berlin painting the dramatic outburst of grief on the part of John and Mary Magdalene has given way to silent resignation. This simplification of the forms and softening of the outline is also apparent in two drawings on the same theme, a sketch in Basle for the Innsbruck painting, which bears the date 1513, and a drawing in a private collection, which is dated 1515. By studying as well two woodcuts on the same subject, the consistent development of Baldung's style from early apprenticeship to the full maturity of the Berlin *Lamentation* shows up in a telling manner.

The artist, whose family came from Swabia, was born at Weyersheim near Strasbourg. At the age of 18 he began his apprenticeship in Dürer's workshop in Nuremberg. It may have been the patricians of the imperial city who later obtained for him the commission for two altarpieces which he completed around 1507 for Halle Cathedral. One, representing the *Adoration of the Magi* (p. 264), eventually found its way to the Berlin Gallery. While in Strasbourg, of which town he had become a burgher in 1509, he received the important commission for the high altar in Freiburg Cathedral, whereupon he moved to Freiburg and spent several years there, roughly between 1512 and 1517. It was only towards the end of the second decade, when he had completed this major work, that Baldung seems to have painted the *Lamentation*, in which one can detect traces of the imposing Freiburg style, a distinct departure from the late-Gothic resonances of the Innsbruck panel.

Hardly anything is known about the origins of this picture. At one time it belonged to a private collector in southern France. Wilhelm Bode bought it and presented it to the Berlin Gallery in 1907.

HANS HOLBEIN THE YOUNGER, 1497/98–1543
Portrait of the Merchant Georg Gisze. Panel, 96 × 84 cm. Cat. No. 586.

From the objects shown in this portrait it is evident that the sitter was anxious that not only his likeness but also something of his way of life should be presented. A Latin couplet above the merchant's head intimates how faithfully the artist has rendered every aspect of the man: 'What you see here, this picture, shows Georg's features and figure – such is his eye in real life, such is the shape of his cheeks.' Yet it is clear from the very form this couplet takes that the picture is meant to convey more than outward appearances and to underline the humanist milieu in which the merchant wished to be seen. The same mood is implicit in a Latin motto inscribed on the rear wall immediately beside a pair of scales: 'Nulla sine merore voluptas' ('No joy without sorrow').

The merchant is depicted standing in his workroom, behind a table covered with a richly embroidered cloth. Among the many objects on the table and the wall which illustrate his trade, the Venetian-glass vase, containing carnations and other flowers, clearly has a special significance; in the medieval language of symbols the carnation was a sign of betrothal.

From the shelf in the top right-hand corner several keys, signet-rings and a spherical container are hanging, the latter presumably containing string. On the table is a pewter writing-stand with goose-feathers, ink, sand, wax disks and sealing-wax. Beside it are a pair of scissors, a signet-ring and a seal. Near the table's edge, precisely placed in the centre foreground, stands a small table-clock which, together with the fragile glass vase and the perishable flowers, is a reminder of the passage of time, as was the hour-glass in earlier pictures.

The name Georg Gisze occurs frequently and appears several times in various styles of handwriting on the documents attached to the wall. From the letter in the merchant's hand one gathers that he has been corresponding with a brother in Germany. The subject of the portrait, the son of an alderman, was born in Danzig in 1497. Holbein painted him in London in 1532. Three years later Gisze married in Danzig, and we may assume that the portrait was commissioned in anticipation of the marriage.

The painting was in the Duke of Orleans' collection in 1727 and appeared in the inventories until 1788. The collection was exhibited at the Royal Academy in London in 1793 and put up for auction. The Swiss publisher and copper-engraver Christian von Mechel acquired the picture and tried in vain to persuade the Basle Library to buy it. For about twenty years it remained in Switzerland without finding a purchaser, until Edward Solly acquired it at a very low price. In 1821 it found its way into the Berlin Museum with the rest of the Solly Collection.

ADAM ELSHEIMER, 1578–1610
The Rest on the Flight into Egypt. Copper, 37·5 × 24 cm. Cat. No. 2039.

The theme of the *Rest on the Flight* is primarily associated with the northern countries and first came into its own *c.* 1500 during the golden age of German painting. The paintings by Altdorfer (p. 95) and Lucas Cranach the Elder (p. 93) in the Berlin Gallery give the scene a magical, fairy-tale quality. The artist's conception of nature at that period was, of course, quite different from that of today. In the sixteenth century the forest was not seen as romantic, but rather as a place fraught with hidden dangers; a century later, when Elsheimer painted his Holy Family, nothing had changed. The angels and the figure of Joseph, even the treatment of light, were clearly inspired by Altdorfer's pictures, but the way in which the heavenly messengers descend to protect the travellers and light up the dark forest reveals the first traces of Baroque art.

Adam Elsheimer was born in 1578 in Frankfurt-on-Main. His first teacher, Philipp Uffenbach, owned a collection of old German drawings which had been left to him by Grünewald. Here we find a direct link between Elsheimer's youth and the art of the Dürer period. The painter left his home at a fairly early age and went to Venice, where he worked with the Munich painter Hans Rottenhammer. It is presumably to this period that the Berlin painting belongs. Its style betrays the influence of Tintoretto, while the composition is modelled on similar works by Rottenhammer. But, in comparing the two German artists, one is aware of the marked superiority of the disciple, who was not content to accept the formality and smoothness of the late Mannerist school and who tried to inject a new truth into traditional themes. Only when he settled in Rome *c.* 1600 did he find his own conception reflected in the trend towards realism that emanated from the art of Caravaggio. Here he met the young Rubens and became acquainted with the landscape art of the Flemish painters Paul and Matthäus Bril.

Elsheimer's art combined an awareness of nature, which was rooted in old German tradition, with an appreciation of the human body, which derived from monumental paintings of the Renaissance. In his own paintings, however, Elsheimer never abandoned the small format which alone enabled him to continue treating details with such loving care. Although the slow pace at which he worked was criticized by his contemporaries, this did not in any way lessen their admiration of his work. His art, his observation of nature, had an influence that was not confined to Italy but also extended northwards, where Rubens and Rembrandt were also subject to it.

The picture was acquired for the Berlin Gallery from a private collection in Nuremberg in 1928.

JAN VAN EYCK, c. 1390–1441
The Madonna and Child in a Church. Panel, 31 × 14 cm. Cat. No. 525C.

The Madonna, with the Child in her arms, is depicted in a Gothic-style church interior with transept and triforium of the French type. The rays of the sun streaming through the stained glass windows fill the whole interior with a soft light. The view of the choir is partially obscured by a richly ornamented rood-screen, in the gables of which are reliefs representing scenes from the life of the Virgin. Framed by the opening in it are two angels with an open book before the high altar. The figure of the Madonna is disproportionately large and dominates the architectural surroundings, yet all the constituent parts of the cathedral are uniformly proportioned, and are represented in precise detail. Frequent, but unsuccessful, attempts have been made to identify the building.

The key to an understanding of what this picture represents was contained in an inscription on the original frame, which was lost when the panel was stolen in 1875. The text was taken from a medieval nativity hymn, in which Mary is praised as the Queen of Heaven, whose virginity is symbolized by the fact that the beams of light falling from the windows leave her untouched. This explains why the painter devoted so much attention to the sunlight penetrating the interior through the glass panes. Light was regarded as a symbol of God and the Virgin as the temple in which Christ 'took up his dwelling'. The church interior thus serves as a Marian symbol, designed to represent the Mother of God as 'Domus dei' and so justifying her magnified stature in the picture. The medieval Marian liturgy is rich in symbols, which reappear in the Berlin panel. The pearl, like the ruby, the sapphire and the emerald, which feature in her crown, are frequently employed as symbols of the purity of the Virgin.

That the Berlin panel originally formed the left, and only surviving, wing of a diptych is confirmed by two copies dating from c. 1500, both of which have a right wing and show a patron kneeling in prayer and turned towards the left. (Antwerp Museum; Doria Gallery, Rome.) The Antwerp diptych, which a Bruges master painted in 1499 for a Cistercian abbot, seems to be a fairly true copy of both the originals by van Eyck.

From 1430 Jan van Eyck spent the rest of his life in Bruges. It was here, in 1432, that he completed work on the Ghent Altarpiece, which his brother Hubert had left unfinished in 1426. The Berlin Madonna must have been painted before he settled in Bruges, perhaps while he was working in The Hague in the service of Duke John of Bavaria (d. 1425).

In the nineteenth century this panel was in the possession of François Cacault, who had assembled his collection mainly in Italy. The architect Nau in Nantes bought it from him. Later it found its way into the Suermondt Collection, which was purchased in 1874 for the Berlin Gallery.

JAN VAN EYCK, c. 1390–1441
Portrait of Giovanni Arnolfini. Panel, 29 × 20 cm. Cat. No. 523 A.

The sitter is painted half-length with folded arms and a turban-style red hat. The collar and sleeves of his robe are trimmed with fur. In his right hand he holds a letter. The three-quarter view shows an impassive face, strongly modelled and with heavy eyelids. Max Friedländer remarked that the head reminded him of a horse's skull.

Giovanni di Arrago Arnolfini was a merchant from Lucca, who was factor in the firm of Marco Guidecon in Bruges, at that time an important world trading centre. His name is first mentioned in connection with the town in 1420 and he was buried there in 1472. Whilst there is no inscription or documentary evidence to show that the Berlin painting is in fact a portrait of him, the picture known as the 'Betrothal', painted by van Eyck in 1434 and now in the National Gallery in London, strongly supports this supposition for the portrait under consideration bears a striking resemblance to the man in the London painting, which since the sixteenth century has been associated with the name of Arnolfini. True, the merchant Arnolfini had a brother, who also worked in Bruges, and since early descriptions of the London picture mention no Christian name, it could be he who is the subject of the picture under discussion. Nevertheless, the identification with Giovanni is still the most likely answer.

The Berlin portrait was obviously painted later than the betrothal picture of 1434. It shows an older man, whose features have become more set and whose bones are more prominent. The way in which the parts are built up and delineated, the use of light and the treatment of material, are all reminiscent of the portrait of the painter's wife, Margareta, painted in 1439 and now in the Bruges Museum.

This picture was at one time in the possession of the Earl of Shrewsbury and was put up for auction with the rest of his collection in 1857. Three decades later Bode purchased it for the Berlin Gallery in London (Auction J. Nieuwenhuis, 1886).

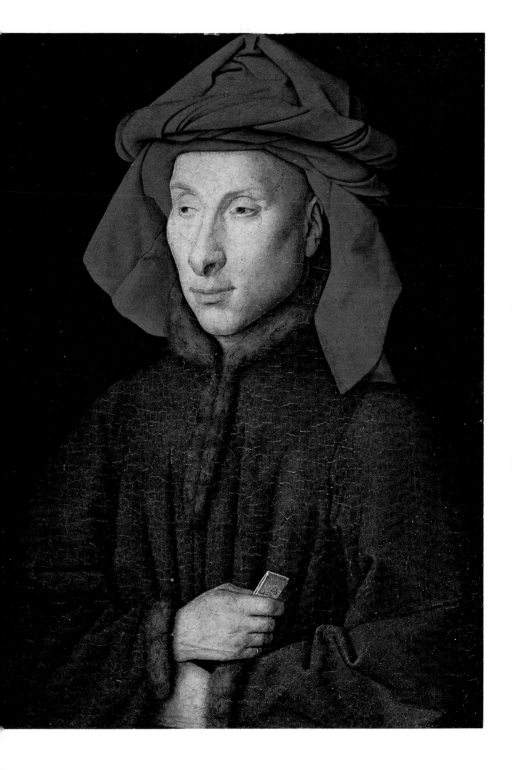

JAN VAN EYCK, c. 1390–1441
Christ on the Cross. Canvas, 43 × 26 cm. Cat. No. 525F.

The Cross stands in a landscape with markedly south European features. The upright of the Cross isolates the two mourners, the Virgin and Saint John, from each other and gives them the appearance of statues. Only the town in the background, which stretches like a frieze before the mountainous horizon, lends unity to the scene. Since the buildings, some of which are domed, and the cypresses and a single pine-tree on the hillside, scarcely suggest a north European town, it is all the more surprising to find here a windmill with its sails outlined against the sky and a great, leafless oak tree, on which birds are settling. As Jan van Eyck travelled to Spain and Portugal in 1428 under the patronage of Philip the Good of Burgundy, it is not unlikely that the impressions he gained there were reflected in the landscape of the Crucifixion.

In his naturalistic approach to the subject, the painter has left nothing to the imagination. The distorted features of the dying man with his matted hair are reproduced in the same precise detail as the utter nakedness of the body, which the transparent loin-cloth does nothing to conceal. A stream of blood gushes from the wound in Christ's side and is joined at the foot of the Cross by a further flow issuing from His forehead. Drops of blood from the nailed hands fall upon the mourners. The ground, on which a few bones are lying, has cracked in many places. The painter was thus following the text of St Matthew's Gospel (xxvii, 51–2), which speaks of an earthquake at the hour when Jesus died.

The realism and immense power contained in this small panel are characteristic features of the new style which Hubert and Jan van Eyck, creators of the Ghent Altarpiece, developed and which marked a clean break with the decorative, graceful art of the turn of the century. Their powers of observation were sufficiently wide-ranging to enable them to depict both ugly reality and the poetry of nature. Certain differences of style between the Berlin *Crucifixion* and Jan van Eyck's known works have led to some speculation as to whether this painting should not be attributed to the elder brother Hubert (d. 1426). But one must not underestimate the capacity of such a great artist as Jan van Eyck to develop his style. The Crucifixion panel must date from about the same period as the Ghent Altarpiece, which was begun in 1425: there are certain details – such as the cloud-formation and the flora – common to both which bear this dating out.

Scarcely anything is known about the origin of this picture, which was purchased from an English art-dealer in 1897. The technical condition of the painting, which was originally on panel and was subsequently transferred to canvas, points to a special process which was practised by Russian restorers and suggests a possible former Russian owner.

PETRUS CHRISTUS, c. 1400–post 1472
Portrait of a Young Lady. Panel, 28 × 21 cm. Cat. No. 532.

The sitter's tall black hat, trimmed with gold braid, is fastened with a broad ribbon under her chin. Round her neck is a triple chain of gold joined with pearls. The low-necked dress is trimmed with white fur and the décolletage is covered by a film-like fabric. A panelled wall serves as a background.

The delicate face with pale lips and slanting eyes, the long neck set above narrow shoulders, lend this beautiful young woman a somewhat exotic air and represent an ideal female type that is not too remote from modern taste. Her captivating appearance has given rise to much speculation as to her identity; it is commonly felt – particularly when comparing her with the types portrayed in other works by van Eyck – that the lady cannot possibly be of Netherlandish origin but is far more likely to be English. A certain Lady Talbot and the wife of Edward Grimeston are among the names mentioned, but to this day the lady's true identity remains a mystery.

When the picture was acquired by the Berlin Gallery, it was still in its original frame, which was subsequently removed for reasons unknown. According to Waagen, it bore the inscription: 'Opus Petri Christophori'. Although he clearly misread the last word, there is no reason to doubt the authenticity of the inscription as such.

Petrus Christus was accorded burgher's rights in Bruges in 1444, three years after Jan van Eyck, his artistic forerunner, died there. Here Petrus Christus was to succeed the greater master and not infrequently even had to undertake copies of works by van Eyck. Max Friedländer, the great connoisseur of Netherlandish painting, was highly critical in his judgment of Petrus Christus's work and even described his relationship to van Eyck as 'parasitic'; regarding the Berlin portrait he wrote, 'the painter's poor sense of form helps to reinforce the impression of feminine charm and the artistic inadequacy of the body strengthens the impression of budding youth.' While this may be acceptable as valid professional comment, the fact remains that we owe to Petrus Christus perhaps the most fascinating female figure in early Netherlandish art.

Nothing is known of the past history of this picture. It was acquired, together with the rest of the Solly Collection, by the Berlin Gallery in 1821.

ROGIER VAN DER WEYDEN, 1399/1400–1464
Portrait of a Young Woman with Coif. Panel, 47 × 32 cm. Cat. No. 545 D.

The young woman, with her expansive Flemish winged or horned coif of fine linen, through which the forehead remains visible, fills almost the entire canvas. The 'nakedness' of the face and the softness of the features form an attractive contrast to the firm outlines of the stiffly folded linen and the dark background. The sitter's hands with beringed fingers are laid firmly one on the other and rest on an invisible sill, support being provided visually by the frame.

The artist came from Tournai and is sometimes known as Roger de la Pasture. There are conflicting reports of his youth and early years. By 1436 at the latest he had become Town Painter in Brussels, an office he held until his death. While in his twenties he married Elisabeth Goffaerts, a native of Brussels, and it has been generally assumed that she is the subject of the Berlin portrait. Although there is no real foundation for it, this is a not unreasonable assumption; the open, warm-hearted expression seems to preclude an official portrait and to suggest someone close to the artist. 'This portrait is full of life and lacks that restraint which ambition, fear of God and custom imposed upon Rogier's representation of human beings' (Friedländer).

It was undoubtedly this impression of intimacy created in this portrait – it occurs nowhere else in the painter's work – which seemed to call for some explanation. To portray the subject looking directly at the viewer was something quite new when this painting was executed *c.* 1435; in the Netherlands this technique occurs for the first time in van Eyck's portraits. The resemblance to the portrait of a woman by Robert Campin, Rogier's teacher, now in the National Gallery in London, is worth noting. The artist has modelled his subject with sympathy and sensitivity, while avoiding contact with the observer. One is left with the feeling that Rogier's art as a portrait-painter began here.

Nothing is known of the early history of this picture. In 1908 it was acquired from an English art-dealer and is believed to have been previously in private ownership in Russia.

The Bladelin Altarpiece. Centre-panel, 91 × 89 cm., wings, each 91 × 40 cm. Cat. No. 535.

In the centre panel the donor is shown kneeling in an attitude of prayer beside the Virgin and Joseph, adoring the naked Child. In the background is a town, perhaps representing Middelburg, near Bruges. The stable of Bethlehem resembles the ruin of a Romanesque chapel. The painter may have had in mind the remains of the palace of King David, who was reckoned among the forbears of Jesus. In the foreground the building is supported by a single pillar which bulks so large beside the tiny figure of the Child that it must obviously be regarded as symbolic. It can be interpreted both as a symbol of sublime power and of the place where Christ was later scourged.

The message of the centre panel alone would be incomplete without the scenes portrayed on the two wings. The three panels together are an allegory of the world dominion of Christ and show not only the ruler of Middelburg and Brabant but also kings in both west and east paying homage to the Child. Tradition has it that, on the day of Christ's birth, a prophetess, the Sibyl of Tibur, showed the Emperor Augustus a vision of the Child and his Mother in the heavens. Here the ruler of the West (the Duke of Burgundy) falls humbly on his knees, removes his crown and swings a censer as a token of sacrifice. In the right-hand wing the three kings of the Orient are depicted, deeply moved and fearful, also kneeling before the vision in the heavens; this is the star of Bethlehem, which appears in the clouds with the embodiment of the Child, to guide them on their journey.

Not only in terms of the subject matter but also in the formal composition of the work, the painter has related the side-wings to the central scene. In so doing, he abandoned the unco-ordinated scheme of the multipartite altarpiece familiar throughout the Middle Ages. One need only compare earlier works by Rogier van der Weyden – such as the tripartite Altarpiece of Saint John the Baptist (p. 269) – to realize the extent of his advance. The bold use of space which the painter makes in each individual scene of the Saint John triptych becomes even more marked in the Bladelin Altarpiece, where the compass of the picture extends over all three panels, and this is also reflected in the abandonment of any dividing architectonic framework.

Rogier was one of the first great painters of the north to visit Italy. Around 1449/50 he must have been in Ferrara, Florence and Rome; and it would have been soon after his return from the south that he received Peter Bladelin's commission. There are few indications of Italian influence in the Middelburg Altarpiece. It is perhaps to be traced in the left wing, where the attendants, standing stern-faced and silent at the picture's edge, recall Quattrocento portraits in Florence.

Peter Bladelin (d. 1472), Treasurer to the Duke of Burgundy and founder of Middelburg, donated the altar triptych to the town church. It has been replaced by an early copy; the Berlin Gallery bought the original panels in 1834 from Nieuwenhuis in Brussels, who had previously purchased them in Middelburg.

SIMON MARMION, c. 1430–1489
The St Omer Altarpiece (detail). Panel, 56 × 147 cm. Cat. No. 1645 A.

Guillaume Philastre, Bishop of Toul and Abbot of St Omer, commissioned the artist in 1453 to paint the wings for an altar-shrine which he donated to the monastery church in 1459. Here this precious work remained until the French Revolution, when the shrine disappeared in the wave of iconoclasm, but the wings were saved.

As the altarpiece was destroyed, the original form it took remains uncertain. The central shrine appears to have been adorned with sculptures wrought in gold and silver. The two wings take the form of a predella, and the original outer surfaces (now at the back) are decorated with grisaille paintings. The artist's major work, however, was the coloured 'open' side extending across both panels, and dedicated to the life of St Bertin, the founder and patron-saint of the monastery church. In two series of five scenes, which are separated by ingenious architectural vistas, the life of the Benedictine monk is depicted from his birth to his death, including his induction, the construction of the new monastery, his miracles and his temptations. In this devout narrative the donor of the panels himself was bound to appear. He had himself portrayed kneeling with a chaplain and clearly identifiable by his escutcheon. The two wings are reproduced on p. 267.

The detail reproduced here shows several monks, who have gathered in the cloister – under a statue representing Saint John the Baptist – to hear a sermon. In the background is an early Gothic cloister, around the walls of which is a continuous painted fresco representing a dance of death. In the far background a young man can be seen leaning against a pillar and admiring the frescoes.

With their subtle use of light and shade and the brilliance of their colours, these panels rank among the finest surviving examples of early French painting. Simon Marmion came from Amiens and from 1458 onwards worked in Valenciennes. In his use of colour and rendering of detail, he modelled himself on Jan van Eyck; the natural ease with which he tells his story and the miniature-like quality of his painting reveals a master of book-illustration. What is particularly surprising is the apparently effortless way in which he overcomes the spatial problem of the cloister, integrating a background which consists of two distinct architectonic elements. This is one of the few pictures from this period that manage to convey both the interior of a medieval cloister and its wall-paintings.

At the beginning of the nineteenth century the wings entered the collection of William II of Holland. They were eventually inherited by the Prince zu Wied, who sold them to the Berlin Gallery in 1905.

JEAN FOUQUET, *c.* 1420–1481
Estienne Chevalier with Saint Stephen. Panel, 93 × 85 cm. Cat. No. 1617.

Estienne Chevalier, who came from Melun, was French Ambassador to England in 1445 and six years later became Treasurer to Charles VII of France. He presented the diptych, of which this panel forms the left wing, to his native town; on this wing he had himself painted next to his patron saint, Stephen. The saint, wearing a deacon's robe, is holding a book, on which a jagged stone is lying, as a symbol of his martyrdom. The formal architecture in the background is in the Italian Renaissance style showing pilasters with coloured inlaid marble panels between them. On the wall, receding in perspective, the name Estienne Chevalier is inscribed several times. Originally the donor and the saint were looking towards the Madonna, who occupied the right wing of the diptych; this panel found its way, as part of the Ertborn Collection, into the Antwerp Museum.

According to a description of the paintings by Denis Godefroy in 1661, the original frames were covered in blue velvet. Round each picture were strands of gold and silver thread, in which the donor's initials were woven in pearls. There were also gilded medallions on which stories of the saints were represented.

Tradition has it – and there is considerable supporting evidence – that the Madonna's features are those of Agnes Sorel, the beautiful and influential mistress of Charles VII. Known portraits of her certainly do not conflict with this hypothesis. Her relationship with Estienne Chevalier was not entirely political, and an eighteenth-century inscription on the back of the Antwerp panel tells us that the diptych of Melun was endowed by Estienne following a vow he made on her death in 1450.

The date of Agnes Sorel's death is not the only reason for assuming that the diptych was painted around 1450. At any later period the cut of Estienne's robe would no longer have been in fashion. A few years earlier, between 1443 and 1447, Fouquet had been in Italy and the background of the Berlin panel is clearly the result of what he saw there. After returning from the south, he settled in his birthplace, Tours. From then on he worked for Charles VII and the court and became the leading exponent of the French Court style.

The diptych was in the chancel of the Church of Notre Dame at Melun, south of Paris, from 1461 until about 1775, when the two halves became separated. For a time the left wing was in Munich, until it passed into the hands of M. Brentano-Laroche in Frankfurt-on-Main. In 1896 it was purchased from his family for the Berlin Gallery.

DIRK BOUTS, *c.* 1415–1475
Christ in the House of Simon. Panel, 40·5 × 61 cm. Cat. No. 533 A.

The story of Jesus's visit to the house of Simon the Pharisee is told in St Luke's Gospel (vii, 36–50). A woman from the city followed Christ there, 'and stood at his feet behind him weeping, and began to wash his feet with tears, and did wipe them with the hairs of her head, and kissed his feet, and anointed them with the ointment.' Simon condemned the attitude of his guest, saying: 'This man, if he were a prophet, would have known who and what manner of woman this is that toucheth him; for she is a sinner.' Christ answered with a parable and the words: 'Her sins, which are many, are forgiven; for she loved much; but to whom little is forgiven, the same loveth little.'

In a narrow, vaulted room, on the left of which is a window providing a glimpse of a landscape, Simon sits with his guests at a table laid for a meal. On the left of the table the sinner bends down to anoint Jesus's feet. The host, the only one present wearing shoes, and Peter beside him, observe the incident with astonishment and disapproval. The youthful John at the head of the table seems to be drawing the attention of the donor, a Dominican monk, to it. The latter kneels with hands raised in prayer and, as if he dare not look, averts his gaze.

The arrangement of the figures at a laid table recalls two other themes from the life of Christ, the Last Supper and the Miracle at Emmaus, incidents which were frequently represented in painting and, furthermore, established a pictorial tradition of their own. Here the table is laid with bread, wine and fish, the last of these being an ancient Christian symbol. The composition of the various objects represents one of the most delightful still-lifes in old Netherlandish painting. Among the vessels on the table one can recognize a late medieval form of glass known as a 'cabbage-stalk'.

Dirk Bouts came from Haarlem, where he doubtless received his early training. Later he settled in the university city of Louvain, where his major work can still be seen in the Church of St Peter. When he was appointed City Painter in 1468, he was already over fifty years old. The Berlin panel, as its close likeness to the work of Aelbert Ouwater suggests, must have been one of his earlier works. This picture, which was at one time in a private collection in Turin, was purchased for the Berlin Gallery in 1904 from the A. Thiem collection.

AELBERT VAN OUWATER, mainly active c. 1440–1460
The Raising of Lazarus. Panel, 122 × 92 cm. Cat. No. 532 A.

The story of the Raising of Lazarus at Bethany, near Jerusalem, is told in the Gospel of Saint John (xi, 1–44). Jesus is taken by Mary and Martha to the grave of their dead brother and asks for the stone to be removed. When Jesus calls out the dead man's name in a loud voice, Lazarus leaves the cave, 'bound hand and foot with grave-clothes'.

Ouwater transfers the incident to the chancel of a romanesque church. The naked Lazarus is sitting on the grave-stone over the open grave, while Jesus, the two women and several disciples stand on the left. Peter, in the centre of the picture, turns with an eloquent gesture of the hands towards the Jews standing on the right and draws their attention to the miracle. Two Jews have raised part of their garments to their faces to keep out the smell of putrefaction, for, according to the Bible, Lazarus had been dead for four days.

The capitals of the pillars between the windows of the chancel are carved with reliefs of biblical stories, scenes from the Old Testament such as the sacrifice of Isaac, which the painter or his patron has linked with the incident portrayed. In other words, Ouwater did more than simply tell the story; the real theme of this picture is the confrontation of believers and unbelievers with death. The key is to be found in the words with which Christ comforted Martha: 'He that believeth in me, though he were dead, yet shall he live . . .'.

The Raising of Lazarus in Berlin is the only one of Aelbert Ouwater's works which – thanks to Carel van Mander's detailed description – can be certainly attributed to the Haarlem artist. It must have been painted c. 1450, at a time, in fact, when Holland had not yet produced any painters of her own to compare with the brilliant galaxy of Flemish artists. One feels, indeed, that Ouwater's rather sober style bridged the gap between the richness of van Eyck's creations and the early works of Dirk Bouts and Geertgen tot Sint Jans in Haarlem.

According to Carel van Mander (1617), who saw only a copy of this picture, it was in Haarlem and was part of the loot carried off by Spanish troops in 1573. Not until 300 years later was it rediscovered and identified thanks to van Mander's description. It is said to have been in the collection of Philip II of Spain, and subsequently the Marchese Manelli inherited the work from the Balbi family in Genoa. Bode acquired the painting for the Berlin Gallery in 1889.

HUGO VAN DER GOES, *c.* 1437/40–1482
The Adoration of the Magi. Panel, 147 × 242 cm. Cat. No. 1718.

The Virgin, with the Child on her lap, is shown seated before a ruined wall. Before her kneels the first of the kings, who approach from the right; Joseph, also on bended knee, adopts a deferential attitude towards the distinguished guests. Behind him one has a glimpse of the Flemish village-square, in which grooms are tending the horses.

This Netherlandish altarpiece, at one time attributed to Rubens, was formerly in the remote monastery of Monforte de Lemos in northern Spain, founded in 1593 by the Archbishop of Seville, Rodriguez de Castro, who is believed to have been the donor of the altarpiece. Although the panel still retains its original frame, it is not quite complete. The roof has been cut off in such a way that in the centre only part of the lower garments of two flying angels are now visible. Heavy forged hinges at the sides of the frame once carried wings; these have disappeared and seem to have been missing while the altarpiece was still in the Monforte monastery. Originally this picture probably adorned a Netherlandish church. Admiration for this work led a number of Flemish artists to copy it or borrow individual motifs. It is from such copies that we know the composition of the lost wings, the *Nativity* on the right and the *Circumcision* on the left, scenes from the childhood of Christ, which constitute the principal theme.

Hugo van der Goes became a Master in his native town of Ghent in 1467. In 1478 he entered the Rooden monastery in the forest of Soignies near Brussels as a lay-brother. He died there four years later, symptoms of mental illness having become apparent some time before his death. Considering the relatively few years he devoted to painting, he left some impressive work behind him. The Monforte Altarpiece is the earliest of his surviving works and must have been painted *c.* 1470. The artist – it may be he who is portrayed on the right next to the Moor – had already gained a high reputation, as he went on to paint a second large altarpiece (now in Florence) commissioned by Tommaso Portinari.

The striking feature of *The Adoration of the Magi* is a freedom of composition and a grandeur which are found in hardly any other early Netherlandish painting. Van der Goes was the first artist in the Netherlands to paint on a large scale and bring power and vitality into his works. It is hard to imagine how an artist who was not familiar with the 'monumental' painting of Italy could portray the impressive figure of the Moorish king, but whether the Ghent master was ever in the south we do not know.

The panel was purchased from the Monforte monastery in 1914.

HUGO VAN DER GOES, c. 1437/40–1482
The Adoration of the Shepherds. Panel, 97 × 245 cm. Cat. No. 1622A.

The Virgin and Joseph are kneeling – almost symmetrically placed – on either side of the crib which, viewed end-on, adds depth to the scene. Angels are crowding round behind the crib in order to be near the Child. Through an opening in the wall in the right background one has a glimpse of the shepherds in the fields, receiving the glad news. On the left side of the picture, two of them rush in, baring their heads as they enter. The entire scene is revealed to the observer by two prophets in the foreground, who draw the curtains back and create the illusion of 'unveiling' it.

The unusually wide yet shallow format of the picture has given rise to the suggestion that it may have been originally designed as a predella. But such an assumption would presuppose an altar of enormous dimensions, the existence of which could not have remained completely unknown. Besides, there is no evidence of predellas in Netherlandish painting, so for the time being the artist's purpose must remain a matter of conjecture.

In his *Adoration of the Shepherds* the painter created something that is far removed from his earlier work, the Monforte Altarpiece. There the composure and dignity of the kings and the natural simplicity of their bearing contrast sharply with the commotion and crowding of the later work, which gives the impression of being somewhat contrived. There is no doubt that the format prescribed by the patron presented the painter with problems of form which were not easy to solve.

Hugo van der Goes painted this work in the closing years of his life, presumably a decade after the Monforte Altarpiece, after he had retired in 1478 into a monastery near Brussels as a lay-brother. The peculiar flatness of the faces and the contrived nature of the whole composition are symptomatic of his later period, in which transitory motifs also become prominent. Although this panel may lack the cohesion of the Monforte Altarpiece, one can still detect in it – particularly in the undignified instrusion of the shepherds – a bold and final attempt by a great artist, who was close to death, to break with accepted tradition in painting and strike out along a new path.

In the middle of the nineteenth century this picture was in the gallery of the Infante Don Sebastian in the castle at Pau (southern France) and was also exhibited from time to time in the museum in Madrid. After his death in 1875 the painting remained in the possession of his wife Maria Cristina of Bourbon, from whose estate it was acquired in 1903 in Madrid for the Berlin Gallery.

GEERTGEN TOT SINT JANS, c. 1465–1495
Saint John the Baptist. Panel, 42 × 28 cm. Cat. No. 1631.

Saint John is shown sitting on a ledge of rock in a summer landscape. Near him lies a white lamb with a nimbus. A brook winds its way between hillocks, and in the distance one can detect the towers of a town. His head supported on his hand – a medieval gesture of sorrow – the Baptist meditates on the Passion of Christ, symbolized by the presence of the lamb, 'which bears the sins of the world'. A striking feature is the placing of the feet which might be interpreted as a reminder of Christ's death on the Cross. The brook recalls the waters of the River Jordan, with which John baptized Jesus. If to the modern eye the landscape seems strangely idyllic, it should be remembered that in the Middle Ages this would have been a dangerous place, devoid of human life and inhabited only by wild animals. Thus when John is described in the Bible as a preacher in the wilderness, this can refer equally to the wilderness of the forest.

There is a surprising degree of freedom and poetry in the treatment of the landscape in this small panel. In the art of Haarlem landscape always plays a special role, and not only in the 'Golden Century' of painting. Ouwater had already become famous for his landscapes, but these have not so far been identified. Dirk Bouts introduced scenes from nature into the background of his pictures. It remained for Geertgen to place his central figure in a natural setting and to integrate it with the background of the green valley, and in so doing he outshone his older compatriot. The landscape is not merely a form of incidental illustration but contributes directly to the mood of the meditating figure.

The painter's name – 'little Gerrit, who lives with the Order of St John' – gives us an indication of where he lived in Haarlem. As this Order was dedicated to the Baptist, Geertgen may well have been commissioned by them to paint the picture, which was intended for private devotions. Little is known of the painter's short life. Carel van Mander reports (1618) that he was a pupil of Aelbert van Ouwater and died at the early age of 28.

At one time in the possession of the English painter W. Cope, this work later passed into the collection of Percy Macquoid in London, from which it was acquired for the Berlin Gallery in 1902.

HIERONYMUS BOSCH, c. 1450–1516
Saint John on Patmos. Panel, 40 × 26·5 cm. Cat. No. 1647A.
Signed: Jheronimus

Saint John is shown sitting on a ledge with an open book on his knee and a quill-pen in his hand. On the hill behind him stands an angel, pointing to a vision in the heavens: 'And there appeared . . . a woman clothed in the sun, and the moon under her feet and upon her head a crown of twelve stars' (Revelation, xii, 1). The Evangelist was at that time regarded as the author of the Book of Revelation and the vision described there taken to refer to the Virgin.

At the saint's feet lie his writing instruments; to the left of him sits a bird, which has been variously described. Its small size makes it unlikely that it is an eagle, the bird usually symbolizing the Evangelist; legend also had it that John kept a partridge as a domestic pet. Opposite the bird and staring at it malevolently sits a fabulous creature with the head of a man and the body of an insect. It belongs to that fiendish family whose members appear in hundreds in the painter's œuvre. In the background stretches a broad expanse of landscape with the estuary of a river as its central feature. It suggests the Rhine valley near Nijmwegen or Arnhem. The luscious green meadows and river banks give an impression of utter tranquillity, yet directly below the vision in the heavens a burning ship can be discerned.

A second painting appears on the reverse side of the panel; here, arranged around a circular central subject – a pelican – are depicted the Stations of the Cross. The pelican, which was said to rip open its breast in order to feed its young with its own blood, was regarded from early Christian times as a symbol of the death of Christ.

Hieronymus Bosch came from the Dutch town of s'Hertogenbosch, which belonged at that time to the Duchy of Brabant. All the information available suggests that he spent his entire working life in this town. It was here that he received important commissions from princely patrons. There is an element of fantasy in his pictures which is so highly individualistic, and his themes are so macabre and cryptic, that the interest of art-collectors was very soon aroused. Amongst these was Philip II of Spain (1527–98). He collected a number of the artist's major works, which are still in the Prado in Madrid. The Berlin panel is one of the very few that bear the master's signature.

The picture was purchased from an English art-dealer in 1907, having previously been in the W. Fuller Maitland Collection in London.

JAN GOSSAERT (MABUSE), 1478–1532
The Agony in the Garden. Panel, 85 × 63 cm. Cat. No. 551 A.

The Gospels describe how Jesus after the supper with his disciples went out in the night to the Mount of Olives. 'And he was withdrawn from them about a stone's cast, and kneeled down, and prayed, saying, Father, if thou be willing, remove this cup from me; nevertheless not my will, but thine, be done. And there appeared an angel unto him from heaven, strengthening him.' (Luke xxxii, 41–43.) Here the artist depicts the night-scene in the wan light of the moon. Christ kneels, pale-faced, in prayer. An angel has set a chalice with the Host on a rock before him. In the background the towers of Jerusalem are just visible in the darkness, and only the arms and armour of the approaching soldiers reflect the light. On the stony ground in the foreground the disciples are sitting or lying, 'sleeping for sorrow'; on the right is Peter, and beside him the sword with which he will later cut off the ear of one of the soldiers.

The picture, which Gossaert painted *c.* 1510, is – like Altdorfer's *Nativity* (p. 265) – among the earliest known night-scenes. No doubt the Antwerp master, who had returned from Italy in 1509, was proud to demonstrate his virtuosity in the use of light and shade and to have created such a palpably realistic illusion in the treatment of his subject. The delicate blending in his style of painting is still in the tradition of the fifteenth century, but in his search for effect he comes very near to artifice. One example of this is the slightly later *Madonna and Child* (p. 271), the frame of which is painted in an illusionist manner. It is significant that in adopting such methods the artist was pandering to the taste of the nobility, for whom most of his work was done.

In the eighteenth century this picture, then attributed to Albrecht Dürer, was in the famous collection of the town-captain of Leipzig, Gottfried Winckler, who possessed nearly 1,000 paintings, in addition to copper-engravings and drawings. His house, which was open to the public, was visited by many of his contemporaries. Goethe paid several visits to the collection not only while he was a student but also later from Weimar and wrote about it in *Dichtung und Wahrheit*. After Winckler's death in 1795 the collection was broken up, but there are watercolour copies which provide evidence of how the originals were exhibited in the collector's house. The painting was purchased for the Berlin Gallery in 1848.

PIETER BRUEGEL THE ELDER, *c.* 1525–1569
Two Chained Monkeys. Panel, 20 × 23 cm. Cat. No. 2077.
Signed and dated: BRUEGEL MDLXII

Under a stone arch, the depth of which suggests that it is part of some fortification, two long-tailed monkeys are sitting, chained to a ring. The opening behind them provides a view of the River Scheldt and the port of Antwerp. Perhaps the artist saw this panorama through the window in the roof of Fort Philippe.

In the Middle Ages the monkey came to be regarded as a symbol of man's instincts and of his bonds with the animal world. Though treated as the focal point of the picture, the captive animals may be taken to have a strong political connotation. It is no mere accident that the little creatures chained to the massive fortress-wall are portrayed against the outline of the city on the Scheldt, which at that time was groaning under the Spanish yoke; the association of ideas cannot have been lost on the artist's contemporaries.

The painted symbol, whether in isolation or artistically linked with other symbols, is a form of expression that was characteristic of Bruegel. The painter and author, Carel van Mander, whose book on the lives of the Netherlandish painters appeared in 1617, maintains that Bruegel, shortly before his death, gave orders for the burning of 'a large number of satirical drawings, which had been duly completed with suitable inscriptions but which in some cases were altogether too biting and steeped in ridicule', because he was afraid their existence might give rise to unpleasant consequences for his wife. The small picture of the monkeys, painted in 1562, a year in which there was a steady growth of opposition to Spanish rule, needed no inscription to explain its meaning.

Bruegel was born in the Dutch village of that name around 1525. His themes are taken from the peasant world and showed life in all its elemental energy and fullness. It is this that explains his popularity. He was the progenitor and at the same time the most outstanding member of a large family of painters. In assessing his paintings merely on their subject-matter, others came to regard him as the 'peasant Bruegel', although he spent all his life in cities, in Brussels and Antwerp. In the dynamism and sensual vitality of his pictures he was the forerunner of another famous Fleming, Peter Paul Rubens, who was born eight years after Bruegel's death.

In 1668 this painting was in the possession of Peter Stevens. This Antwerp collector owned altogether eleven works by Pieter Bruegel, which were the pride of his collection and show how discerning was his taste in pictures. These seem to have included also the other Bruegel painting now in the Berlin Gallery, the *Netherlandish Proverbs* (p. 272), which is even more famous than the *Monkeys*. The latter was acquired by a Russian prince and eventually, in 1931, reached Berlin by way of a Paris art-dealer.

GIOTTO, c. 1266–1337
The Death of the Virgin. Panel, 51 rising to 75 × 179 cm. Cat. No. 1884.

Of this painting Vasari says 'it is a small panel in tempera, on which, painted by Giotto with boundless care, the death of Mary is depicted, with the apostles around her and a Christ who takes the soul of his mother into his arms. This picture has been highly praised by the masters of painting, especially by Michelangelo Buonarotti. He declared . . . that this remarkably conceived representation came as close to reality as is possible in a painting.'

The panel is bounded at the top by a shallow gable, the peak of which serves to emphasize the figure of Christ standing behind the sarcophagus. A great crowd of apostles and angels have assembled to mourn the dead woman. The corpse, laid out on a cloth, is lowered into the marble coffin, while Christ holds the soul of the Virgin, in the shape of a small child, in his arms.

Giotto was born in Colle di Vespignano, a small place north of Florence. Not much is known about his life and his training. Shortly after he began working in Florence c. 1300, he received the important commission to paint the family chapel of Enrico Scrovegni in Padua; this monumental series of mural paintings established his fame throughout Italy. By the time he came to paint the altarpiece of the Death of the Virgin, Giotto had emancipated himself from the limitations imposed by mural painting with its substantial forms and figures set within predetermined flat surfaces. Despite the compact grouping of the composition, in which 43 persons are included, the main figures evoke emotions such as no painter before Giotto had succeeded in expressing. The frequently discussed question whether this panel was the work entirely of his own hand or whether a workshop made some contribution is immaterial, for, at the time it was created, the authorship of a work of art was judged quite differently from today.

In describing what is almost certainly this panel, Lorenzo Ghiberti (d. 1455), in vol. II of his *Commentarii*, and Vasari, in the first edition of his *Lives* (1550), both referred to it

136

as being in the Ognissanti Church in Florence. It obviously did not remain in the church for long after 1550; by 1568, when the second edition of Vasari's work appeared, it was no longer there. Not until the nineteenth century did it reappear, when it was put up for auction in 1845 as part of Cardinal Fesch's collection. It then passed into the possession of the Davenport-Bromley family at Wooton Hall, where it was at the time of its acquisition in 1914 for the Berlin Gallery.

MASACCIO, 1401–1428
The Martyrdom of St Peter. Panel, 21 × 29 cm. Cat. No. 58 B.

The panel reproduced here belongs to the predella of a multipartite altarpiece. It was commissioned by the notary Giuliano di Colino degli Scarsi and was painted by Masaccio in 1426 for the Chiesa del Carmine in Pisa. The altarpiece was dismantled not later than the seventeenth century; its various parts are now scattered among a number of different art-collections. Several found their way to the Berlin Gallery, among them the adjacent predella panels showing the martyrdoms of Saint Peter and Saint John the Baptist.

Vasari saw the altar and in the second edition of his *Lives* he described it as follows: 'In the Chiesa del Carmine in Pisa he created in the chapel of the transept a panel-painting, a Madonna and Child with a few small angels making music at her feet, one of the angels listening intently to the harmony of the notes. Beside the Madonna are Saints Peter, John the Baptist, Julian and Nicholas, all figures full of life and move-ment. In the predella he represented on a smaller scale incidents from the lives of these saints and in the centre the three Magi, worshipping Christ . . . In the upper part of the painting are several pictures with many saints gathered round a crucifix.'

This description made it possible to rediscover the greater part of the panels over the last hundred years and to reconstruct the altar. Especially noteworthy are the two largest paintings, the *Crucifixion* now in Naples and the *Madonna Enthroned* in the National Gallery in London. The *Adoration of the Magi* (p. 275), which Vasari particu-larly admired, formed the centre-piece of the predella, while the *Crucifixion of Saint Peter*, together with the *Beheading of Saint John* were probably situated to the left of it.

The painter portrays the martyrdom of the saint, who was crucified upside-down, with stark realism. The execution takes place in a narrow courtyard, with several soldiers carrying shields on guard. The symmetrical arrangement of the body, with vertical and horizontal axes parallel to the sides of the picture, and the arms stretched between the two walls give the whole conception the proportions of a monumental painting. The dominating size of the figures in this small panel makes it a precursor of Masaccio's major work, the frescoes in the Brancacci Chapel in S. Maria del Carmine, which marked a turning-point in fifteenth-century Florentine painting.

The panels were purchased from the collection of the Marchese Gino Capponi in Florence for the Berlin Gallery in 1880, together with the *Adoration of the Magi* from the same altarpiece.

SIMONE MARTINI, 1284–1344
The Entombment of Christ. Panel, 22 × 15 cm. Cat. No. 1070A.

The mourners are gathered round the body of Christ, which the Virgin cradles in her arms over the open sarcophagus. The disciples kiss the hands and anoint the feet of Jesus. Mary Magdalene, her fair hair hanging loose, throws up her arms and wails aloud; John, weeping, covers his face. In the background palm-trees and orange-trees stand out against the evening sky.

This tiny panel, the size of a small book, once formed part of a small altarpiece, the other parts of which are now scattered among various collections. Four of them, representing the Archangel Gabriel, the Annunciation, the Crucifixion and the Descent from the Cross, are in the Antwerp Museum; one showing Christ carrying the Cross is in the Louvre. Like these, the Berlin panel originally had a gold ground, over which the landscape was later painted. This alteration – intended to create a sense of illusion – is in striking contrast to the flattish, tapestry-like nature of the composition.

We do not know who commissioned this little altarpiece. In the *Descent from the Cross* a kneeling bishop is depicted as donor. It has been suggested that this was Cardinal Jacopo Stefaneschi, because he commissioned other works from Simone, but on the back of the panel in the Louvre is the coat of arms of the Orsini, which would suggest rather that the donor was one of the bishops from that Roman family. There are therefore several possibilities.

Simone Martini was a younger contemporary of Giotto and, after Duccio, the leading exponent of Sienese painting. He was much in demand as an artist, and also received commissions from outside Siena (Naples, Pisa, Assisi, Orvieto, Florence). In 1339 he moved to Avignon, where he worked for the Papal court until his death. It is generally assumed that this small altarpiece was produced during this period, since all the panels from it were purchased in France. On the other hand, the Gothic-style expressionistic features seem to suggest an earlier period, which may have some connection with Simone's work in Pisa and the influence of Giovanni Pisano.

Little is known about the provenance of this painting, which was purchased for the Berlin Gallery in 1901 from a private owner in Paris (Emil Pacully).

FRA FILIPPO LIPPI, c. 1406–1469
The Virgin adoring the Child. Panel, 127 × 116 cm. Cat. No. 69.
Signed: Frater Philippas P.

The author of the Medici inventory of 1498, where it is first mentioned, devotes only a few lines to a description of this picture – no more than he does to its exquisite frame. The unusual feature of this representation escaped him. The new-born Child lies naked in a woodland meadow, with dense, dark trees forming the background beyond. Between the trees, some of which have fallen or been cut down, flows a stream. A goldfinch (here perched on a tree-stump on the right) is a symbolic motif accompanying the Christ-child also found in other pictures of this period. Its blood-red head and its fondness for thistles makes it a natural symbol for Christ's crown of thorns.

Embedded in a felled tree-trunk in the left foreground is an axe, the handle of which is directed into the picture and bears the painter's signature: immediately above it stands the small figure of Saint John, with a scroll carrying the words: 'Ecce Angnus Dei Ecce qu' ('Behold the Lamb of God . . .'). The association with the wood of the Cross and with the warning of John the Baptist, '. . . the axe is laid unto the root of the trees' (Matthew iii, 10), is fairly clear. We are reminded not only of the divine mission of the Child, on whom the rays of the Holy Spirit are falling, and of the supreme sacrifice which He is destined to make, but also of the sins of the world that caused it.

Fra Filippo, who was put in the care of the Carmelite Order in Florence at an early age, took his vows in 1421. Masaccio's frescoes in the Brancacci Chapel in S. Maria del Carmine are among the works that made a profound impression on the young painter-monk, as did later those of Fra Angelico. Some time after the mid-century he moved to Prato, where he spent more than ten years working on the cathedral frescoes. It was here, around 1458, that he painted the picture we are considering.

At about the same time as Fra Filippo was painting his altarpiece, Benozzo Gozzoli was decorating the small windowless room of the Medici Chapel with gold-gleaming frescoes showing the three Magi and their retinue approaching the worshipping Madonna.

In 1492 this panel was in the family chapel of the Palazzo Medici-Riccardi in Florence. While the Medici were in exile, it was transferred to the Town Hall, where there is a record of it in 1510. With the return of the Medici family, the painting was restored to its original home, where Vasari saw it in 1550. We do not know when it was removed from the chapel. It found its way into the Berlin Gallery as part of the Solly Collection in 1821; its place in Florence has been taken by a contemporary copy.

DOMENICO VENEZIANO, c. 1400/10–1461
Portrait of a Young Lady in Profile. Panel, 51 × 35 cm. Cat. No. 1614.

The painting shows a young woman wearing an exquisite brocade dress. Although at first glance a half-length portrait is suggested, the subject's posture indicates that she is sitting in the marble embrasure of a window or balcony. A bright blue sky fills almost the entire background and contrasts with the pale flesh-tint to give the picture its distinctive colour-harmony.

The painter has shown an incredibly sure touch in bringing out the essential features of the young woman's face in profile. The features are delineated with the minimum of detail. The pattern of the brocade dress, depicted in the plane, underlines the medallion-like character of the picture. The emphatic use of line and the clarity of the contrasting colour-surfaces have always been regarded as typical of the Florentine style, but opinions differ as to the identity of the master.

The attribution to Domenico Veneziano we owe to Wilhelm Bode; before he purchased the portrait it had been attributed to Piero della Francesca. Admittedly, almost nothing is known about Domenico's life-history. His name suggests Venetian extraction, yet he spent most of his working-life in Florence. Among the few works which can be safely attributed to him is the altar for S. Lucia dei Magnoli in Florence (now in the Uffizi), of which the Berlin Gallery possesses a predella panel (p. 276), but the style of painting employed there is difficult to reconcile with the chiselled lines of the Berlin portrait. Latterly, therefore, the view has gained ground that this portrait was the work of Antonio Pollaiuolo (1433–98). He was a versatile Florentine artist, who, in addition to painting, ran a goldsmith's workshop and also produced designs for embroidery.

The portrait was purchased in 1894 for the Berlin Gallery from the Earl of Ashburnham's collection.

LUCA SIGNORELLI, c. 1441–1523
Portrait of a Jurist. Panel, 50 × 32 cm. Cat. No. 79C.

The portrait is that of a middle-aged man wearing a red cap and a red robe with a black stole over it. In the background are antique buildings, in front of which are two girls in classical garb and two naked youths.

Signorelli came from Cortona, a small mountain-town in the south of Tuscany. Pierro della Francesca, while working on a great cycle of frescoes in nearby Arezzo, appears to have been his, the young Signorelli's, teacher. Vasari reports in his *Lives* that the pupil had so mastered the style of Piero 'that one could not distinguish one from the other'.

Signorelli must subsequently have been in Florence, for the clarity of the draughtsmanship in his figures comes very close to the style of Verrocchio and Pollaiuolo. He also shared their interest in depicting the nude; the accurate rendering of anatomical detail plays an important part in the foreshortening and movement revealed in Signorelli's work. Despite a certain Gothic angularity, his nudes exude a spirit of the antique, just as the background of this portrait is full of antique 'quotations'. It is reasonable to assume that these were included in response to the wishes of the subject, who was anxious to provide visible evidence of his humanist background. It is also possible that the commission for the Berlin portrait, which was probably painted c. 1490, was only given to Signorelli on account of his skill as an anatomical draughtsman. In an important commission from Lorenzo the Magnificent, c. 1488, the painter had had an opportunity to demonstrate his skill. This was the famous *Pan*, one of the major works in the Berlin Gallery which was among the irreplaceable masterpieces lost during the Second World War.

Formerly in the Casa Torrigiani in Florence, this painting was purchased from a Florentine art-dealer for the Berlin Gallery in 1894.

ANDREA DEL CASTAGNO, 1423–1457
The Assumption of the Virgin. Panel, 150 × 158 cm. Cat. No. 47A.

The Virgin, her eyes turned towards heaven, is depicted seated in the mandorla, in the form of a cloud borne by four angels. She is dressed as a nun and her hands are raised in prayer. On either side of the cloud, which has the appearance of crystalline rock, stands a saint: Saint Julian on the left holds a sword in his hand; on the right the martyr-king Miniatus, patron saint of the church for which the work was painted, leans in an elegant posture on the mandorla. Roses and lilies are growing in the empty marble sarcophagus in the foreground. The thirteenth-century *Legenda Aurea* records that the apostles who had carried the Virgin to the grave were, on the Assumption of the Mother of God, suddenly surrounded by flowers, the red roses here proclaiming the presence of martyrs, the white lilies that of angels and virgins.

The sharp clarity of line and the modelling of the figures are reminiscent of a work of sculpture. In fact, there is a relief by Donatello in Naples (S. Angelo a Nilo), which is devoted to the same theme and which seems almost to anticipate Castagno's handling of it. The sculptural realism of the figures, on the other hand, is in marked contrast to the unreality of the subject, particularly where the painter treats the insubstantial cloud as if it were a solid object. The gold background of the picture merely strengthens the impression of paradox, which may partly account for the fact that it took so long to establish the painter of this panel. Only in 1910, with the advance in knowledge of the technique of Quattrocento art and the discovery of documents relating to the period, was it possible to identify the altar-panel as one of Castagno's attested works.

Among the masters of the Quattrocento in Florence, Castagno occupied a special place insofar as he personally succeeded in adapting certain stylistic elements of the older generation to the ideas of his own time. From the beginning his compositions were monumental in outline and form; his gifts were soon recognized and brought him commissions in Venice while still a young man. Here, in the early 1440s, he painted frescoes in the dome of S. Zaccaria and completed a mosaic in St Mark's. After his return to Florence (1444), he designed a *Descent from the Cross* for a glass painting in the cathedral there. In the sheer size of his figures, the sharply chiselled lines and the glowing predominantly red and gold colour scheme, which are the outstanding features of the Berlin painting, Castagno adapted his monumental style to panel-painting and combined the spirit of late Gothic art with the ideals of Botticelli and his generation.

This altar-panel was painted in 1449 to a commission from Leonardo di Ser Francesco Falladanzi for the church of S. Miniato fra le Torre in Florence. It was repeatedly described as being here up to the eighteenth century, for example by Vasari in 1550, by Baldinucci in 1681 and by Richa in 1754. When the panel was removed from the church is not known, but it was certainly not later than 1785, when the building was demolished. In 1821 it found its way into the Berlin Museum with the Solly Collection.

BOTTICELLI (SANDRO FILIPEPI), 1444/5–1510
The Virgin and Child with Singing Angels. Panel, tondo, diam. 135 cm. Cat. No. 102A.

The Child, held by the Virgin on her lap, is depicted trying to open her dress while turning his head towards the viewer. Standing on either side of the Madonna are four angels carrying white lilies. Only one of them, on the extreme left, is looking – like Mary and Jesus – straight out of the picture. The sadness, entirely of this world, shown in all the faces is heightened by the unreality of the background. The lilies rise like flames into the blue of the firmament, in which two hands can be seen holding a crown over the Madonna's head.

For the Florentine masters of the Renaissance the tondo as an art-form was a constant source of interest. Botticelli's attempts to combine the Marian theme with the tondo form were all made during his earlier period. Two related panels in the Uffizi in Florence make an interesting comparison and give us an insight into the formal problems which confronted the artist in adopting the circular shape. In the Berlin Madonna the artist had adapted the composition to the round form by grouping the angels in such a way as to harmonize with the shape of the panel – as does the posture of the Child – while at the same time framing the Virgin in a kind of niche. In spatial terms the problems of composition have been resolved purely by means of draughtsmanship; in this Botticelli achieved an expression of extreme sensitivity and lyricism.

Count Athanasius Raczynski (1788–1874), a Polish diplomat in Prussian government service, bought the Madonna tondo in 1824 in Paris from a Monsieur Revil, who, as Napoleon's War Commissioner, had brought it back with him from Italy. The work thus found its first home in Berlin in the Palais Raczynski, which was situated near the Brandenburg Gate. In 1884, when the house was demolished to make way for the new Reichstag building, the Count's collection was exhibited for a time in the National Gallery on the Museum Island and then, in 1903, transferred to the Landesmuseum of Posnania, a Prussian province; an exception was made in the case of the Botticelli tondo, however, which at Bode's instigation was presented by the count's family to the Kaiser-Friedrich Museum on permanent loan. Fifty years later the painting was finally purchased for the Berlin Gallery.

BOTTICELLI (SANDRO FILIPEPI), 1444/5–1510
Saint Sebastian. Panel, 195 × 75 cm. Cat. No. 1128.

Sebastian was a Roman officer who was condemned to be shot by bowmen because of his Christian faith. As he survived the execution, his martyrdom was regarded as a parallel to Christ's crucifixion. Botticelli gave this parallel artistic expression by portraying the saint bound to a tree, standing on the remains of two severed branches, high above a landscape with riders and foot-soldiers. The height of the tree can only be guessed from the depth of the background, since the base of the trunk is not included in the picture. The painter creates a strangely moving effect by placing the observer on a slightly lower, though unreal, plane and by fixing the martyr's eyes firmly upon him.

According to an anonymous contemporary source, Botticelli painted the panel in 1474 for S. Maria Maggiore in Florence, where it was originally displayed on the first pillar of the south aisle. In the first edition of Vasari's *Lives*, which appeared in 1550, the painting is still mentioned as occupying the same position. When it was removed from the church is not known. It must be assumed that the nature and height of the panel's original setting in S. Maria Maggiore influenced the composition. Though the young Botticelli conformed to Gothic traditions, these origins are overshadowed by the artist's southern feeling for the rendering of the human body and his precise knowledge of anatomy.

Fra Filippo Lippi, Verrocchio and Antonio Pollaiuolo were Botticelli's real teachers. The latter two especially influenced the young artist, who had previously worked in a Florentine goldsmith's shop, and left their mark on the style of the Berlin picture. It is interesting to compare this work with Pollaiuolo's roughly contemporary Saint Sebastian altar in the National Gallery in London. The dramatic and varied portrayal of horror shown there is alien to Botticelli's style. His art lies essentially in the beauty of form; his conception is conditioned above all by the treatment of the contours.

In 1821 this work came into the possession of the Berlin Museum as part of the Solly Collection.

PIERO DI COSIMO, 1462–1521
Venus, Mars and Cupid. Panel, 72 × 182 cm. Cat. No. 107.

'He also painted a picture with a naked Venus and a Mars, who has laid down his arms and now sleeps naked on a flower-covered meadow. In addition one sees various putti, which are dragging the greaves and other weapons of Mars hither and thither. Further one sees a myrtle-grove, a Cupid frightened by a rabbit, the doves of Venus and other attributes of the goddess of love. The picture hangs in Florence in the house of Giorgio Vasari, who preserves it as a memento of the artist, whose singular flashes of genius always give him joy.' With these words Vasari perpetuated in his *Lives* (1550) the memory of Piero di Cosimo's picture.

The artist's treatment of the subject may have been inspired by the poetry of Angelo Poliziano, who was a friend of Lorenzo de' Medici; the latter is also known for his sonnet on a similar theme. However, the composition and mood of the picture recall a work of Botticelli's in the National Gallery in London, and we can safely assume that this work also helped to inspire Piero's painting.

The Florentine artist gave of his best in his representations of profane subjects. Although this very inventiveness produced a slightly naïve effect, and despite a certain smoothness of line, he was one of the first in Florence to develop a genre entirely his own; in the case of religious subjects, however, he achieved little that was original. His predilection for mythology and profane allegory was in keeping with a somewhat bizarre way of life, which Vasari describes. In Florence wide use was made of his outstanding talent to design fantastic masquerades and ceremonial processions.

After Vasari's death in 1574 the painting found its way to the Casa Nerli in Borgo San Niccolo, Florence. Carl Friedrich von Rumohr, who described it as the 'best of the master's works known to me', purchased it in 1829 for the Berlin Gallery.

RAPHAEL, 1483–1520
The Virgin and Child with Saint John. Panel, diameter 86 cm. Cat. No. 247A.

The Virgin is shown seated with the Child on her lap before a hilly landscape. On her right stands Saint John grasping a scroll of paper, which Jesus holds in His hands. The scroll bears the words: 'Ecce Agnius Dei' ('Behold the Lamb of God'). The child on the Virgin's left is believed to be Saint James the Less, although he bears no particular identifying characteristics. In the background a hill-town can be seen.

Raphael, the son of a goldsmith, was born at Urbino. After an initial period as pupil of Timoteo Viti, he went to Perugia at the age of sixteen to continue his apprenticeship with Pietro Perugino. Two works from that period which were clearly influenced by his master are the *Madonna* from the Solly Collection and the *Virgin and Child with two Saints* (p. 278), both now in the Berlin Gallery.

In the autumn of 1504 the young painter was drawn to Florence, where the presence of Leonardo and Michelangelo had given a new stimulus to the artistic life of the city. In the next four years, until he finally settled in Rome, he worked alternately in Perugia and Florence. The work we are considering here, a painting of homely simplicity, must have been produced at the beginning of this period.

It has been said that it was only after he went to Florence that Raphael developed into the Madonna-painter we know. There he mastered the art of combining the element of 'monumentality', a quality peculiar to that city, with a quite unpretentious style of human intimacy and simplicity. The composition lacks the skill of Botticelli (see p. 151) and seems to pay scant attention to the round format of the picture. The concept of the seated woman in a landscape and her demeanour towards the children have no precedent. This rural family idyll is far removed from the divinely radiant Madonna of earlier times; it shows her as Savonarola saw her in his sermon: 'The Blessed Virgin was a woman of the people, and simply dressed.'

This picture was at one time in the possession of the family of the Duke of Terranuova, who had residences in Genoa and Naples; it was purchased from the family in 1854 for Berlin.

FRANCESCO DEL COSSA, c. 1435–1477
Allegory of Autumn. Panel, 117 × 72 cm. Cat. No. 115A.

The picture shows a peasant-girl; she carries a spade, a hoe and two branches bearing grapes, all of which pertain to viniculture. The figure is seen slightly from below, backed by a hilly landscape with a low horizon. A river runs through the meadows, which skirt a town, and near the bridge several horsemen can be seen. The landscape is believed to represent the neighbourhood of Sassuolo (not far from Modena) at the foot of the Apennines.

This mundane theme is treated in such an imposing manner as to lift it into the realm of allegory. The girl has set one foot on a stone step, which partly conceals the other foot and at the same time forms the bottom edge of the panel. This illusionist effect gives the figure a statuesque quality, an impression which is reinforced by the classical Greek tunic, the *chiton*, which the girl is wearing. It comes as no surprise to learn that the artist also worked as a sculptor and was compared to the Greek masters by his contemporaries.

One is tempted to regard this picture as one of an imposing series of seasonal allegories such as are found in medieval illuminated manuscripts. Since the Baroque period the Berlin panel had served, together with other allegorical pictures, as a room decoration. The paintings, which today are scattered among several museums (Budapest, Florence, London, Milan), originally formed part of the interior decoration of quite different rooms. The Berlin picture may be the only one that survived from an entire seasonal series.

It is reasonable to assume that the *Allegory of Autumn* is a work by Cossa dating from c. 1470. About this time he also painted seasonal pictures for the frescoes of the Palazzo Schifanoia at Ferrara, his birthplace. We find the closest parallel to his imposing, statuesque figures in the art of Piero della Francesca. According to Vasari, Piero, who came from Umbria, worked at various times for the ducal Court in Ferrara. Here Cossa would have had an opportunity to study Piero's style, the influence of which is apparent in his works.

Formerly in the council-chamber of the Palace of the Inquisition near S. Domenico in Ferrara, this painting became part of the Costabili Collection there in the nineteenth century, when it was attributed to Cosimo Tura. In 1893 it was sold in Milan (Barbacinto auction) and was purchased the following year for the Berlin Gallery.

ANDREA MANTEGNA, 1431–1506
The Virgin with Sleeping Child. Canvas, 42 × 32 cm. Cat. No. S 5.

The Virgin is dressed with the utmost simplicity; below her head-cloth, several strands of hair hang loose. With her hand she holds the sleeping Child tenderly to her breast. A golden cloak embroidered with a pattern of pomegranates enfolds Mary and the Child like a shawl. The Child is tightly wrapped in swaddling-clothes, so that only the head and hands are visible. This may have been customary at the time, but it is rather suggestive of a corpse wrapped in winding-sheets. There is a possibility that the painter intended an allusion to the death of Christ, and in the action of the mother holding her son to her breast anticipated the representation, which later became widespread, of the *Pietà*, depicting Mary with the dead Christ on her lap.

This small picture must have been painted during Mantegna's early years, as it was inspired by similar subjects in Donatello's work, such as his stucco relief formerly in the Berlin Museum, which was one of the works destroyed in 1945. The young painter must have met the Florentine sculptor, while he was working in Padua (1443–53). Mantegna's *Presentation of Christ in the Temple* (p. 278), likewise in the Berlin Gallery, must also belong to his Padua period. In style it is very close to the Madonna and there are marked similarities in the treatment of the Child and of the garments. Both pictures are painted in tempera on canvas, a medium not often used at that time. We learn from a letter written by the artist in 1477 that he recommended his patron to order pictures painted on canvas, as they could be rolled up and more easily despatched.

The first we hear of Mantegna is when, at the age of ten, he became the pupil and adopted son of Francesco Squarcione, a painter of local repute who lived in Padua; of the latter's few signed works one is in the Berlin Gallery. The young artist spent six years in his teacher's workshop, but he undoubtedly absorbed much of the atmosphere of the busy university town. He was only seventeen years old when he finally parted company with his master and received his first important commission, the altar for S. Sofia in Padua, which has since been lost.

This picture, which at one time was in the collection of the Conte della Porta in Vicenza, was acquired from an English art-dealer by James Simon. A great patron of the arts, he presented his collection to the Berlin museums in 1904; included in it was this Mantegna painting, which was placed in the Kaiser-Friedrich Museum.

ANTONELLO DA MESSINA, c. 1430–1479
Portrait of a Young Man. Panel, 20 × 14 cm. Cat. No. 18.
Signed and dated 1478

The young man is shown gazing quizzically at the observer. His soft features are framed in dark-brown hair partly covered by a black cap with a hat-band hanging from it. The green landscape behind him is dominated by a deep-blue sky. On the stone sill along the bottom of the picture the painter has incorporated his signature apparently on a piece of paper: 'Antonellus Messaneus me pinxit' ('Antonello from Messina painted me'). Beneath it, in golden letters which cover the entire breadth of the panel, is inscribed in Latin the motto: 'In good fortune be modest, but in adversity prudent'.

Antonello spent the greater part of his working-life in his native Messina. He assimilated the art of the Netherlands, particularly that of the brothers van Eyck, more thoroughly than any other Italian painter, and adapted it to his style. Yet, so far as we know, he never crossed the Alps. Southern Italy, especially Sicily, was ever responsive to northern influence. Not only had Sicily belonged to the Kingdom of Castile since 1412, but the Spaniards had occupied Naples while Antonello was still a young man. Spanish culture, which already bore the imprint of Netherlandish art, became dominant in southern Italy and prevented an Italian school of painting from taking root. At the court of King Alfonso of Aragon Netherlandish painting played a significant role and his collection contained pictures by Jan van Eyck and Rogier van der Weyden.

Naples seems, moreover, to have been the city in which Antonello acquired the basic ingredients of his art. His earliest surviving work, the *Crucifixion* in Sibiu (Hermannstadt), Rumania, is based on a composition by Jan van Eyck. This influence remained with the Sicilian throughout his life, without however impairing his own artistic development and individual style. The Berlin portrait of 1478, though the last of his signed and dated works, still bears the hallmarks of this tradition, and yet here too one can detect impressions which the painter had gained shortly before, during a visit to Venice.

In 1773 this portrait was in the Vitturi Collection in Venice. Later it was purchased by Edward Solly, from whom it was acquired in 1832 – after he had settled in London – for the Berlin Gallery.

GIOVANNI BELLINI, *c.* 1428–1516
The Dead Christ. Panel, 82 × 66 cm. Cat. No. 28.

Giovanni Bellini was the youngest and most distinguished member of a family of
Venetian painters of the fifteenth century. Trained in the workshop of his father,
Jacopo, he was also influenced by Andrea Mantegna, who was about the same age
and who became his brother-in-law in 1454. Among Bellini's favourite themes, to
which he returned again and again, were representations of the Madonna and the
Lamentation in which the figure is shown half-length – a treatment already accorded
the subject by Donatello. It provided the artist with an opportunity to combine a
careful and subtle study of the nude with an expression of muted pain. Here Bellini
succeeded in giving visual expression to new spiritual realms which no one before him
had made manifest.

Two angels are supporting the naked body of the crucified Christ, who is sinking
back from a sitting position. Each holds the dead man's arms with one hand, while
their faces lean gently against his head. Bellini had previously executed two paintings
on the same theme; one is now in the museum at Rimini, the other in the National
Gallery in London. In the first of these, which is in landscape format, there are four
angels. This rather too fanciful interpretation was abandoned in the London picture,
which – making the most of the upright format – shows Christ with only two angels.
It was not until he painted the picture now in the Berlin Gallery, which cannot date
from before 1480, that Bellini succeeded in achieving a composition which has balance
in a classical sense, and in which the natural beauty of the human body is completely in
harmony with the spiritual content of the subject. At the same time, the graphic
structure of the picture with its soft yet vigorous contours loses none of its prominence,
and in this the likeness to the art of Mantegna is unmistakable. It is hardly surprising
that precisely this style should have deeply impressed Albrecht Dürer, the draughtsman,
and that, during his visit to Venice, he wrote of Bellini that he was 'still the best of all
painters'.

This picture became the property of the Berlin Gallery in 1821 with the rest of
Edward Solly's Collection.

VITTORE CARPACCIO, *c.* 1455–1525/26
The Entombment of Christ. Canvas, 145 × 185 cm. Cat. No. 23 A.

In the foreground of a rocky landscape the body of Christ is laid out on a stone table, behind which a bearded man is seated, leaning against a tree and sunk in grief-stricken meditation. In the background three men are removing the stone door from a burial chamber hewn into the rock, in preparation for the burial. On a pathway which runs deep into the landscape Mary can be seen supported by a woman, together with John, both overcome by grief. The quiet beauty of the dead body and the bucolic atmosphere of the summer landscape are in startling contrast to the grim details of the burial-place, which bears all the traces of devastation. The account in St Matthew's Gospel (xxvii, 51–2) of the death of Christ seems to explain the scene: 'And the earth did quake and the rocks rent; and the graves were opened; and many bodies of the saints which slept arose'. No literary source has so far been found to explain the man sitting by the tree; he is commonly taken to be Job, the long-suffering patriarch of the Old Testament. In the stone table, on which Christ was laid for the anointing, one recognizes the so-called 'red stone', which was venerated in the Middle Ages as a sacred relic and is still preserved in the Church of the Holy Sepulchre in Jerusalem.

As a 'story-teller', Carpaccio was more prolific and more colourful than any of Venice's Renaissance painters. In his choice of subjects he showed a marked preference for lesser-known themes which lent themselves to colourful treatment, and for an architectonic type of scenery, viewed through the eyes of a painter, in the style of his teacher Gentile Bellini. Even in his early work, the series of pictures from the life of Saint Ursula (Venice, Accademia), which he began in 1490, his remarkable talent as a story-teller was already apparent. The mysterious Berlin *Entombment* with its combination of horrifying and lyrical detail is a typical example of the painter's epic genius. It was painted *c.* 1505, about the same time as Carpaccio was producing his cycle of paintings for the Scuola di San Giorgio in Venice.

When in the Canonici Collection in Ferrara in 1627, this work was attributed to Mantegna. In fact, it still bears an old, but false, signature: 'Andreas Mantinea f.'. The Berlin Gallery acquired the picture in 1905 through the Kaiser-Friedrich Museum Society.

LORENZO LOTTO, *c.* 1480–1556
Portrait of a Young Man. Canvas, 47 × 37·5 cm. Cat. No. 320.
Signed: L Lotus pict.

This portrait of a bearded man in white lace collar and black cap derives its impact from the bright red curtain which serves as a background. The cloth, which is drawn slightly to one side and draped carelessly over the parapet, allows a glimpse of the sea receding to the horizon.

Among the copper-engravings of works in the Giustiniani Gallery, which were published in 1812, this picture is described as a self-portrait. Whether the author of the book was basing this statement on some family tradition or some inscription which has since been lost, we do not know. The features of Lorenzo Lotto, as represented in other pictures, would certainly not conflict with this identification. The glimpse of the sea, on which several ships and white sails are visible, has led to the alternative suggestion that the subject might have been connected with shipping and not therefore the painter himself.

Lorenzo Lotto, whose family came from Bergamo, was born in Venice. The first artists to influence him were Giovanni Bellini and Alvise Vivarini. He soon left Venice to carry out commissions in various towns, particularly in northern Italy. Between 1509 and 1512 he was working in Rome. In addition to large altar works, in which Mannerist features are already apparent, he produced a number of important portraits which show a high degree of psychological characterization. Three of Lotto's portraits in the Berlin Gallery attest to his skill in this field; he conveys the moulding of the features in the Venetian style by means of light and shade rather than line. The contours of the head are reproduced with a soft brush and set against a coloured background.

This portrait must have been painted *c.* 1530. The whole conception of the painting recalls Titian, who was of the same generation as Lotto and was on friendly terms with him. The work was formerly in the Giustiniani Collection, which was put up for auction in Paris in 1815 and was acquired by the Berlin Gallery.

SEBASTIANO DEL PIOMBO, *c.* 1485–1547
Portrait of a Young Roman Lady. Panel, 76 × 60 cm. Cat. No. 259B.

The young woman, wearing a kerchief on her head, is depicted looking directly at the observer. With her right hand she gently holds in place the fur-lined velvet cloak draped loosely over her shoulder, while her left hand rests on the handle of a basket of fruit. To the left of the picture behind her is a window through which one can see a hilly landscape bathed in evening light.

The earlier assumption that this was a portrait of Raphael's mistress is untenable, for there is little or no similarity to the so-called 'Fornarina' in the Palazzo Barberini in Rome, and furthermore this latter portrait cannot be said with certainty to be a faithful likeness. On the other hand, the style of painting and the kind of kerchief the sitter is wearing would justify the title of 'Roman lady' for the Berlin picture.

As early as 1832 Passavant had refused to accept the picture as a Raphael, although a copy in Verona (Castello Vecchio) had been attributed to Raphael as long ago as 1657. Waagen was the first (1835) to detect the hand of Sebastiano and his attribution has not been contested since.

The affinity with the art of Raphael is understandable, when one considers the Venetian painter's background. He received his first training in the workshops of Giovanni Bellini and Giorgione, but it was the latter who had the greater influence on his style of portraiture. Following Giorgione's death in 1510, Sebastiano received a commission from Agostino Chigi to work with Raphael on the interior decoration of the Villa Farnesina and he moved to Rome. Although his work on this imposing scale did not come up to expectations, his reputation as a portrait-painter grew.

Sebastiano must have painted the Berlin portrait at the beginning of his Roman period, for Raphael's influence is already apparent; he was then at his artistic peak. The similarity of style between it and his portrait of a woman, dated 1512, in the Uffizi at Florence, which has also been wrongly described as the 'Fornarina', has always been remarked upon. Here too the graceful treatment of the cloak betrays the artist's Venetian origins, just as the atmosphere of the landscape beyond the 'Roman lady's' head reveals the continuing influence of Giorgione.

In the eighteenth century this picture was in the possession of the Duke of Marlborough. Thomas Chambars published an engraving of the painting in 1765 under the title 'Raphael's Mistress', and another by John Boydell appeared in 1796 in a published collection of the most famous pictures in England. In his memoirs Bode describes the efforts he made to acquire for Berlin the outstanding works in the Blenheim Palace Collection, which were put up for sale in 1884 and which included this portrait.

GIORGIONE, c. 1478–1510
Portrait of a Young Man. Panel, 58 × 46 cm. Cat. No. 12A.

The portrait shows a young man with dark, shoulder-length hair; the subject's eyes are fixed on the observer, his right hand rests on a parapet in front of him. The letters 'VV' at the foot of the picture have not so far been explained; among the suggestions put forward have been an abbreviation of the subject's name or a motto (Vanitas vanitatum?).

The painter, who died young, left only a small number of paintings, not a few of which have since been destroyed. His early death, the little we know of him and of his close kinship with Titian, whose work frequently shows a similarity to his, have meant that Giorgione remains a somewhat enigmatic figure. Of the same generation as Raphael, he was the first of the distinguished series of great Venetian masters in the sixteenth century.

Giorgione probably came from Castelfranco and his presence in Venice is confirmed from 1506 onwards. In the following year he worked in the Doge's Palace, in 1508 he undertook a commission to decorate the Fondaco dei Tedeschi, the headquarters of the German merchants in Venice. We do not know to what particular circle the subject of the Berlin picture belonged; the general assumption is that the portrait, which corresponds roughly to the style of the *Madonna of Castelfranco*, was painted c. 1505. Among Giorgione's few portraits, the painting in Berlin is without parallel; it recalls rather the late portraits of his teacher Giovanni Bellini, such as that of the Doge Loredan in the National Gallery in London. It would seem that in this portrait the younger artist expressed for the first time, both in interpretation and style, the individuality of the sitter while at the same time adhering to the classical form of the High Renaissance.

During the nineteenth century this painting was in the Giustiniani Collection in Padua and passed into the possession of Jean Paul Richter in Florence in 1884. In 1891 it was purchased by the Berlin Gallery.

TITIAN, c. 1488–1576
Venus and the Organ-player. Canvas, 115 × 210 cm. Cat. No. 1849.
Signed: Titianus F.

Venus is depicted reclining on a couch, naked but for a veil, which reveals more than it conceals, across her thighs, and wearing bracelets and necklace of precious stones. Leaning on a cushion, she has turned her head back, as if to listen to Cupid's words. The tiny god of love clings to her shoulder and with his left hand reaches towards her breast. At the foot of the couch, seen only from the knees up, sits an elegantly-dressed nobleman at an organ.

The motif of the recumbent nude with a cavalier sitting near her is one that Titian employed in several paintings of similar composition (Madrid, New York, Cambridge). As the persons depicted have varying and quite individual characteristics, these works would appear to be double portraits, in which courtesans and their lovers are represented. This group of pictures has obviously so much in common, that the question has constantly been asked how the artist came to adopt this particular style in the first place and what the prototype was. In 1548 Titian sent a 'Venus' from Venice to Augsburg, where the Emperor Charles V was in residence for a meeting of the Imperial Diet. (Two years earlier, he had promised the Emperor to deliver a painting on the same subject.) Later the picture was sent from Augsburg to Madrid. In 1567 another consignment of Titian paintings, which again included a 'Venus', was despatched to Philip II of Spain in Madrid.

It was in keeping with the taste of the Imperial Court that the Venus motif should no longer be bound up with mythology but should be made topical by introducing the organ-player. The features of the elegant cavalier with the reddish-brown hair are those of Philip II (1527–98). If this is really the son and heir of Charles V, who was then not yet twenty-five, then only he, or someone in his immediate entourage, would have commissioned the Berlin picture. It has never been established whether the identity of the reclining beauty was immediately apparent to the artist's contemporaries, but, however that may be, the artist's treatment of the group must have seemed quite unprecedented and erotically challenging.

Titian raised the 'banal motif', as Bode once called it, above the level of everyday life into an arcadian sphere. The red curtain behind Venus' head, the fine cloth draped over her couch and even the barking dog, which seems to be holding the observer at bay, convey something of the intimacy of an interior, which, at the same time, is offset by the broad expanse of landscape beyond. Many features of this landscape in itself, as it were framed by the two figures, indicate that the artist, in his understanding of nature, was some fifty years ahead of his time.

Little is known about the provenance of this picture. Until 1914 it is believed to have been in Italy in the possession of the Spanish branch of the House of Orleans. In 1918 it was purchased for the Berlin Gallery in Vienna.

TITIAN, c. 1488–1576
Portrait of a Daughter of Roberto Strozzi. Canvas, 115 × 98 cm. Cat. No. 160A.
Signed and dated: Titianus f. Annor II MDXLII

The girl, who, according to the painter, was two years old, is shown wearing a long silk dress; she stands by a marble balustrade, holding out a pretzel to a small dog. There seems to be something spontaneous about the way in which child and animal have looked up and both pairs of eyes, dark and expectant, have a strangely moving affinity. The precious jewellery the child is wearing marks her social status, for her parents came from the most distinguished families in Florence, the Strozzi and the Medici.

There is some doubt as to which of Roberto Strozzi's daughters is portrayed in Titian's picture. The available evidence suggests that it would have been the eldest, Clarice, of whom little is known except the dates of her marriage and death. The poet Pietro Aretino (1492–1556) saw the painting immediately after it was completed and wrote to the artist on 6 July 1542: '. . . such a work is no less difficult to comprehend than it is to make, and it deserves to rank above all pictures not only of the past but also of the future . . . I would praise the small dog, which she is caressing, if cries of admiration at the trueness to life, which inspires it, were sufficient. And so I close, for I am speechless with wonder'. The poet's words express his admiration not only for the beauty of the painting but also for its 'trueness to life'. There are few examples in sixteenth-century portraiture of a child as the sole subject. The artist's contemporaries must, therefore, have been all the more surprised by the child's lack of self-consciousness as she plays with the animal, for there is little doubt that the artist fulfilled all expectations in producing a faithful likeness.

This portrait was painted in 1542 in Venice, where Roberto Strozzi, the child's father, had lived since 1536 and married three years later. He subsequently moved to Ferrara and finally to Rome, where the picture must have taken its place in the Strozzi family's palazzo. It was once publicly exhibited around 1641 in the porch of S. Giovanni Decollato. At the beginning of the nineteenth century it was transferred to the family palazzo in Florence, where Bode acquired it for the Berlin Gallery in 1878.

CORREGGIO, c. 1494–1534
Leda and the Swan. Canvas, 152 × 191 cm. Cat. No. 218.

The love-saga of Jupiter, who, in the form of a swan, consummated a union with Leda, was an erotic theme that commended itself to many artists. Another of the love-affairs of the Father of the Gods, the story of Danaë, was the subject of a painting by Correggio, commissioned by Duke Frederick II of Mantua (Rome, Villa Borghese). The painter, who in his early years was inspired by Mantegna and Leonardo, had been working since 1518 in Parma, where he created a sensation with his bold, illusionist ceiling-paintings. The way in which he conveys light and the sensual modelling of his figures are features of the baroque style, of which he was to that extent a forerunner, and it is hardly surprising that appreciation of his art reached its peak in the eighteenth century.

Very few great paintings have had such a varied history as this work, which was sought after by almost all the European ruling houses. Frederick II of Mantua, who commissioned this painting c. 1530, presented it to the Emperor Charles V. It remained in the possession of the Habsburgs for some time. It is mentioned in the inventory of the estate of Philip II of Spain (d. 1598). In 1603 the Emperor Rudolf II, who when still a young prince had admired it in Madrid, transferred it to his residence in Prague. During the Thirty Years' War Swedish troops occupied the Bohemian capital and in 1648 removed the picture as war-booty to Stockholm.

Queen Christina of Sweden, who had amassed an art-collection, refused to be separated from her pictures on her abdication (1654) and moved the *Leda* to her residence in Rome. In 1722 the painting again changed hands. The Regent of France, Philip of Orleans, brought it to Paris, but his son Louis was so provoked by the picture that, in a fit of religious frenzy, he slashed the canvas. The Inspector of the art-collections, the Court painter Charles Coypel, succeeded in saving the work, except for the head of Leda which had been completely ruined; he undertook the task of restoring the painting and replacing the missing area. The picture reappeared as part of Coypel's estate and found its way into the Pasquier Collection. In 1755 Frederick II of Prussia arranged for it to be purchased in Paris and placed it in his picture gallery at Sanssouci. Half a century later it started on its travels again, when Napoleon, after defeating the Prussians, had the painting moved to Paris. In 1815, following Napoleon's downfall, it returned to Berlin, where it was exhibited in the museum at the Lustgarten from 1830 onwards. It was at this period that the restorer Schlesinger, with a sensitivity that must still command our respect today, reworked the head of Leda.

ANGELO BRONZINO, c. 1502–1572
Portrait of Ugolino Martelli. Panel, 105 × 85 cm. Cat. No. 338A.
Signed: Bronzo Florentino

Ugolino Martelli (1519–92) was a scholar from a distinguished Florentine family, whose residence stood near the Palazzo Medici. As a writer he made his name with a tract on Horace. Later he took Holy Orders and was appointed Bishop of Grandèves in southern France. This portrait shows Martelli as a young man seated in the courtyard of his Florentine palazzo, a Renaissance building of noble proportions which has survived to this day. In the background is a marble statue by Donatello, of the young David with the head of Goliath, which only in recent times left the Palazzo Martelli for the National Gallery in Washington; a bronze model for the statue is in the Berlin Museum.

The care with which the ambience is created shows that Martelli wished to be regarded as a person with a humanist education. This is reflected both in his clothes and in the demonstrative posture of the hands. His left hand rests on a book by the Venetian scholar Pietro Bembo (1470–1547), his right on Homer's *Iliad.* The open pages show the Greek text of the ninth canto.

A clue to the date of this picture is the age of the sitter, who can only have been about twenty at the time. The portrait must, therefore, have been painted after 1535. Shortly before this, Bronzino had been working in Pesaro for his patron, the Duke of Urbino, and had won great repute for himself, particularly with his portraits. After returning to his birthplace, Florence, he painted a number of portraits, which in style and delicacy of touch come very close to those of his teacher, Pontormo.

Most of Bronzino's later work was done in the service of the Grand Duke of Tuscany, Cosimo I, and he painted several portraits of his patron and of his wife, Eleonor of Toledo. A portrait of the latter (p. 278), which is now in the Berlin Gallery, must have been painted after their marriage in 1539, shortly after the portrait of Ugolino Martelli. Common to both pictures is the elegant polish of Florentine Mannerism and a cold detachment in the psychological approach.

Although Vasari mentioned this painting in his *Lives,* published in 1550, we know nothing of its whereabouts until the nineteenth century, when it was in the Palazzo Strozzi. In 1878 Bode acquired it for the Berlin Gallery, together with Botticelli's portrait of Giuliano de' Medici (p. 277), Titian's portrait of a daughter of Roberto Strozzi (p. 177) and several rare Renaissance busts.

CARAVAGGIO (MICHELANGELO MERISI), c. 1570–1610
Love Victorious. Canvas, 154 × 110 cm. Cat. No. 369.

The importance of this unusual picture, on a prescribed allegorical theme, was recognized by Caravaggio's own contemporaries. The painter and writer Joachim von Sandrart, who published an authoritative work on German art in 1675, described the painting as 'a life-size Cupid with the figure of a boy about twelve years old, sitting on the globe and holding his bow in his right hand, with, on the left, all kinds of instruments; also books for studies and a laurel-wreath on the books.' Sandrart's matter-of-fact description gives almost no hint of the vitality with which the artist met the challenge and mastered this didactic subject. A naked Roman youth sits, legs wide apart, on a blue globe, which represents the universe, and regards the observer with a smile on his face. His complicated stance is as spontaneous as it is lacking in natural repose.

The posture is reminiscent of a similar treatment by Michaelangelo. But it is precisely when we draw a comparison with the Renaissance conception of the human figure that we realize how far Caravaggio has moved away from it and how uncompromisingly the baroque painter cast aside the idealistic traditions of the past. The harsh light from the left of the picture brings out the contours of the naked body: every wrinkle and fold of the skin is reproduced with the utmost realism.

The revolutionary nature of his art was also reflected in Caravaggio's private life. Naples, Malta, Syracuse, Messina and Palermo all served as places of refuge at various times in his stormy career. Although Caravaggio never left Italy and died at an early age, his work had a profound influence on European painting. The new 'naturalism' of his pictures, their substantiality and the techniques of light and shade he employed made a lasting impression on the painters of the Netherlands.

This painting was commissioned by the Marchese Vincenzo Giustiniani and his brother Benedetto, who became a cardinal in 1586. They were particularly interested in the new realism of Caravaggio's *Amor profano*, which had as its theme the victory of celestial over earthly love. Both pictures, which featured in a lawsuit as early as 1603, were acquired by the Berlin Gallery when it purchased the Giustiniani Collection in 1815.

ORAZIO GENTILESCHI, c. 1565–1639
Saint Christopher. Copper, 21 × 28 cm. Cat. No. 1707.

St Christopher, a man of gigantic proportions, lived by a river and was in the habit of carrying travellers across the water. One day a child asked him to perform this service, but he had the greatest difficulty in reaching the other bank, as the weight of the child seemed to press him down into the water. After Christopher had overcome the dangerous situation, the child, having been set down safely, identified himself: 'Thou has not only carried the entire world on thy shoulders but also Him who created the world'. The painter here depicts the legend with loving care: with his final step the saint reaches the safety of the bank and looks up anxiously at the child, who sits on his back, without holding on, and points with one hand towards heaven. The water glistening in the sunlight, the foliage of the trees and bushes, the stones and grasses on the bank are all portrayed in the finest detail. It is hardly surprising that, for a long time, this picture was attributed to Adam Elsheimer, who painted similar landscapes on copper in Rome.

Gentileschi, the son of a goldsmith, was born in Pisa and went to Rome when he was 17 years old. Here, from the turn of the century, he followed the new trend towards realism which began with Caravaggio and also gained ground among northern artists. Having a special feeling for colour-effects, he managed to avoid the sort of stark contrasts and violent movements which were much sought after by Caravaggio's successors. He always showed a preference for beauty of line and form with occasional lyrical touches. Since the 1920s this small Berlin landscape has been accepted as the work of Gentileschi, although almost all his known compositions are on a large scale. The delicate, poetic way in which the theme is treated and the silvery clarity of the landscape are no less typical of the artist, however, than are the mannered movements of the figures and the effective use of light dervived from Caravaggio.

Nothing is known of the history of this picture before the nineteenth century. There are records to show that it was in private collections in Vienna from 1838 onwards (Joseph Winter collection; Baron Stummer von Tavarock collection). In 1913 it was presented to the Berlin Gallery.

ANNIBALE CARRACCI, 1560–1609
Roman Landscape. Canvas, 80 × 143 cm. Cat. No. 372.

On a river-bank a young couple can be seen playing musical instruments. Several boats are plying on the water. The far bank is built up with stonework laid out in the form of terraces; water cascades from openings in the wall and, beyond, steps lead down to the river. The middle distance is dominated by a citadel-like building erected on a high bastion and connected with the opposite bank by means of a stone bridge with rounded arches.

Annibale Carracci came from Bologna, where he received his earliest training. In Parma he studied the art of Correggio and later he also visited Venice. Cardinal Odoardo Farnese summoned him to Rome in 1595. Here Carracci embarked upon his greatest undertaking, the decoration of the gallery of the Palazzo Farnese, which was to occupy him for eight years.

In the first decade of the seventeenth century Rome was the centre of the most modern currents in artistic development. Landscape-painting took a new and decisive course, particularly under the influence of Paul Bril, Adam Elsheimer and other northern artists, but Annibale Carracci and his pupils also played a vital part in the development of this art-form. Carracci's idea of beauty was, however, different from that of the northern artists; his landscapes bear little relation to reality but present a lyrical picture of nature, in which the carefree behaviour of the human figures and the richness of the elements are interwoven with the solemnity of historical buildings.

The style of the Berlin landscape still reflects some of the impressions which the art of Titian, Tintoretto and Veronese had left on Carracci while in Venice. The prominence of architecture in the composition and the heroic motif of the monumental bridge spanning the river lend the picture a pronounced Roman quality. The artist must have painted it during his early years in Rome.

The painting was purchased for the Museum in 1815 from the painter Bonnemaison in Paris, at the same time as the Giustiniani Collection was acquired.

186

JOHANN LISS, *c.* 1597–1629
The Ecstasy of St Paul. Canvas, 80 × 58 cm. Cat. No. 1858.

In his second Epistle to the Corinthians, St Paul describes the revelations that were made to him. Liss portrays one of the apostle's visions, 'how that he was caught up into paradise, and heard unspeakable words, which it is not lawful for a man to utter'. Above the seated apostle, who is surrounded by books, an angel draws aside a curtain; terrified, Paul shrinks back from the expanse of heaven revealed to him. Angels playing musical instruments gambol in the clouds, and in the distance the Trinity appears. The colours range from the deep violet of Paul's cloak through the green of the curtain to the most delicate yellow, blue and pink of the clouds. This painting with its extraordinary wealth of brilliant colour is one of the artist's finest works and seems to anticipate the Venetian painting of the eighteenth century.

With the exception of Adam Elsheimer, Johann Liss was the most outstanding German painter of the seventeenth century. He was born in Schleswig-Holstein *c.* 1597, spent several years studying in the Netherlands, where he came into contact with the Haarlem painters, principally Goltzius and Buytewech, and with the Flemish followers of Caravaggio in Antwerp (Janssens, Jordaens). Liss then made his way to Italy via Paris. To begin with, he worked in Rome, where he was a member of the Netherlandish artists' colony, and exactly when he settled in Venice is not known. Until his early death, a victim of the plague which broke out in 1629, he continued to work in Venice and it was in these last years that he produced his best-known works, among them *The Ecstasy of St Paul.* Together with Domenico Feti, Liss played an important part in reviving the use of rich colours, a Venetian tradition which had ended with Tintoretto.

In the seventeenth century this painting was in the famous collection of the Amsterdam merchant Gerrit Reynst (died 1658), which consisted mainly of works by Venetian masters and included a companion-piece, *The Vision of St Peter,* which was subsequently lost. Both pictures were engraved by Jeremias Falck and attributed to Johann Liss, but it seems certain that the St Peter picture was not the work of Liss but of Domenico Feti, who was a close friend of the German painter. It may be that after Feti's death (1623), his patron decided to commission Johann Liss to paint the companion-picture to the *St Peter.* *The Ecstasy of St Paul* came up for sale in Amsterdam in 1722 with the Van de Amory Collection and found its way through a Florentine art-dealer into the Berlin collection of A. von Frey, from which it passed in 1919 to the Picture Gallery.

ANDREA SACCHI, 1599–1661
Portrait of Alessandro del Borro. Canvas, 203 × 121 cm. Cat. No. 413A.

An elegantly dressed gentleman of considerable girth is shown standing at the top of a flight of steps. The presence of a massive pillar beside him, coupled with the fact that he is presented above eye-level, help to emphasize the subject's physical appearance. From his elevated position he looks down on the observer. The banner lying on the ground has white and red stripes decorated with golden bees, the emblem of the House of Barberini in Rome. Alessandro del Borro was a general in the service of Duke Ferdinand II of Tuscany and in 1641–43 fought successfully against Pope Urban VIII, head of the Barberini family, for possession of the Castro district.

The identification of the subject with this Tuscan general is not, however, very convincing. It is based on the presence of the Barberini banner lying at his feet, which led to the conclusion that the portrait must be that of an opponent of Urban VIII. Known portraits of Borro show only general resemblances with the Berlin painting, and the patently satirical character of the picture, which represents a Falstaffian figure rather than a general, makes the hitherto accepted identification very dubious. A more likely explanation would be that this is an actor playing some particular role; this theory is supported by the fact that in another painting, by the same artist and of similar size and composition, is in the Los Angeles Museum. In that work an actor is portrayed, and it may thus have some close affinity with the subject of the Berlin portrait.

For a long time this painting was attributed to Velázquez; and was purchased for Berlin as a work by the Spanish master. Only in more recent years has it been attributed, with some reluctance, to Andrea Sacchi. The artist came from the vicinity of Rome, and he worked almost exclusively in that city. He was a pupil of Francesco Albani and became known particularly as a painter of altar-pictures. Pope Urban VIII repeatedly entrusted him with major commissions, a fact which may provide the most likely explanation for the Barberini banner lying on the ground.

Formerly in the Villa Passerini near Cortona, the painting was purchased for the Berlin Gallery in Florence in 1873.

Bathsheba bathing. Canvas, 109 × 142 cm. Cat. No. 454.

The story of Bathsheba is told in the Old Testament (2 Samuel, xi). From the roof of his palace King David sees the young woman bathing. Captivated by her beauty, he has her brought to him and makes her his mistress. When she becomes pregnant, he sends Bathsheba's husband, Uriah, to join his troops 'in the forefront of the hottest battle', so that he shall be slain. The plan having been implemented and Uriah killed, the king marries Bathsheba.

The painter portrays the young woman's bathing-place in luxurious surroundings in the courtyard of a palace. The beauty of the naked body is so much the focal point of the picture that the story is almost irrelevant, and for a time the subject was taken to be the Toilet of Venus. The only clear pointer to the Bathsheba story is the woman in the left background who brings the letter from the king.

The range of colour in the picture, with white, blue, golden yellow and red as the basis, follows in the tradition of Veronese, and yet the free, almost sketchy use of the brush and the rich gradation of tones are also reminiscent of Tiepolo. There is one fundamental difference between them, in that Ricci clings to a classical composition, which goes back to the Venetian masters of the sixteenth century, and manages to employ to great effect a bold decorative style.

Frederick II was not very successful in his efforts to obtain works by Veronese for his picture gallery. None of the paintings attributed to this master have stood up to modern critical analysis, but not all of them suffered as a result. The brilliant painting of Bathsheba, which might have fitted into Veronese's repertoire but does not bear his unmistakable signature, was dismissed as a copy of the Renaissance master by Tiepolo; hence the picture came to be recorded by art-historians as the work of Tiepolo. Only in recent times has the attribution to Sebastiano Ricci been confirmed.

The courtly, often somewhat stylized elegance of Ricci, who was a generation older than Tiepolo, reflects the way of life of a much-travelled artist. In Rome he studied the paintings of Pietro da Cortona, in Milan the works of Magnasco. In 1715 he became a member of the Académie Royale in Paris, and worked both in the Netherlands and in London and Vienna. The Berlin 'Bathsheba' must have been painted during the artist's later years in Venice. That it could be regarded as a work by Veronese a mere generation after his death shows how deeply committed he was to the tradition of that city.

In 1773 this picture (then attributed to Veronese) was in Frederick II's possession; in 1830 it was transferred from the collections in the royal palaces to the Berlin Gallery.

FRANCESCO GUARDI, 1712–1793
Balloon Ascent. Canvas, 66 × 51 cm. Cat. No. 501 F.

On 15 April 1784 a balloon was released over the Grand Canal in Venice, opposite the Piazzetta. The balloon had been built for the procurator Francesco Pesaro, and its pilot was the Conte Giovanni Zambeccari. A year earlier in France the brothers Mongolfier had attempted the first free flight in a hot-air balloon. The première in Venice was a great occasion, which was recorded in copper-engravings and a commemorative medallion. Guardi must also have been influenced by the unique nature of the event which brought crowds of spectators into the streets. He depicts the ascent as seen from beneath a shaded portico, beyond which lies the bank of the Giudecca with Andrea Palladio's Redentore Church. The balloon hovers in the blue sky above a launching-platform erected in the water and surrounded by many gondolas. Ladies and gentlemen, all elegantly dressed, have gathered in large numbers and are watching the flight with rapt attention.

Guardi was the last in the series of great Venetian artists and, apart from Canaletto, its best-known painter of architecture and *vedute*. His views of the lagoon-city, sparkling with light, and his *capricci*, small, imaginary landscapes, brought him fame. He received his training through his elder brother Gianantonio, who had taken over the family workshop after his father's death. In 1719 Francesco's sister married Giovanni Battista Tiepolo, the outstanding Venetian master of the eighteenth century.

Francesco, it would seem, very seldom left his birthplace; for him the city could provide more than enough in the way of stimulus and subject-matter. When he painted his *Ascent* he was already in his seventies. At that time he painted a whole series of 'happenings', all of them filled with people and movement, such as Pope Pius VI's meeting with the Doge, a ball or a gala concert, events which provided the elegant society of Venice with an opportunity to appear in their finery and enabled the painter to display the scintillating treasures of his palette.

Nothing is known about the history of this picture before it was acquired for the Berlin Gallery in 1901.

GIOVANNI BATTISTA TIEPOLO, 1696–1770
The Martyrdom of St Agatha. Canvas, 184 × 131 cm. Cat. No. 459B.

This picture was painted *c.* 1756 for the high altar of the church of S. Agata in Lendinara. It must originally have been rounded at the top, for it appears in this form in an etching by Tiepolo's son, Giovanni Domenico. The part which is now missing showed a heart surrounded by the crown of thorns in a nimbus, at which the saint was gazing. The beautiful Agatha was a devout Christian who lived in Catania. She steadfastly refused to make sacrifice to the heathen gods. When she defied the threats of the Roman Governor of Sicily, Quintianus, he ordered her breasts to be cut off. We see her, half-naked, on a flight of steps; a maid kneels behind her, supporting her and holding her dress against the bleeding wounds. A page stands in front of a marble pillar, holding the severed breasts of the martyr on a silver platter and gazing down at her. The uncouth figure of the executioner, clad in red and holding a blood-stained sword, towers menacingly over the group.

Tiepolo is among the last of the great Venetian painters, a master of large-scale composition, who was commissioned by princes outside (Würzburg, Madrid) as well as inside Italy. Nor did he shrink from this particularly horrifying subject; once before, twenty years earlier, he had been required to treat the same subject for the church of S. Antonio in Padua. With astonishing self-assurance the painter succeeds in portraying this fearful episode in artistic terms without allowing it to degenerate into mere blood-shed and horror. At the same time, so strong is his desire for realism – and he had doubtless witnessed executions himself – that he exploits to the utmost the artistic possibilities open to him.

In colour and form the composition is extremely accomplished, almost too much so to do justice to the theme. Between the soaring pillar and the towering figure of the executioner, one glimpses the dark entrance of the dungeon and beneath it the pale face of the martyr, flanked on both sides – almost oppressively close – by the faces of the two witnesses. The compassion expressed in the attitude of the young woman on the right contrasts with the searching glance of the page on the left, in which merely the physical effect of the scene before him is reflected. The wide, pale-blue cloak of the saint serves to bind the group of three figures together and blends with the silver-white, the bright yellow and the orange to produce a colour-harmony that is characteristic of Tiepolo. Two of the artist's crayon studies for the saint's face are in the Kupferstich-kabinett (Copper Engravings section) in the Berlin Museum.

In the nineteenth century this painting found its way to England, and became part of the Munro collection in London. It was purchased for the Berlin Gallery in 1878.

GEORGES DE LA TOUR, 1593–1652
Saint Sebastian. Canvas, 160 × 129 cm. Cat. No. 2046.

Saint Sebastian, who survived execution by the bowmen of the Roman Emperor Diocletian, is found by Saint Irene after nightfall, and the pious princess and her companions take the seriously wounded man into their care. The scene is illuminated by the harsh light of a torch. The saint lies naked and apparently lifeless by the tree to which he had been bound. An arrow has pierced his chest; the helmet at his feet identifies him as a Roman officer. The woman with the torch kneels by his side and gently holds up one of his arms. The naked flame above the martyr's head – falling back as if in sleep – is a symbol of the life that is still in him.

Sebastian was worshipped as the patron saint who protected people against the plague and his miraculous rescue was regarded as symbolic of the resurrection of Christ. The composition of this picture recalls similar representations of the 'Lamentation', a stock subject that goes far back into the Middle Ages. In his use of light and shade and in the eloquence of the hands La Tour reveals the influence of Caravaggio, whose *Entombment of Christ* (in the Vatican) has impressed many painters. La Tour, who came from Vic-sur-Seille near Nancy, was Court painter to French kings and the town painter of Lunéville, and he enjoyed a considerable reputation as a painter of night-scenes. There is reason to believe that, during his early years as an artist, he was in touch with Caravaggio's Dutch followers in Utrecht, and the night-pieces of Honthorst, who returned from Italy in 1620, with their subtle use of light may well have exerted a particular influence on him.

Two night-scenes by La Tour on the subject of Saint Sebastian are on record, but it has proved impossible to say with certainty which of these is the Berlin painting. One of them was seen by Louis XIII when he was in Nancy in 1632, and he was so impressed with it, that he would have no other picture in his room. The other was already in the possession of Duke Charles IV of Lorraine. The presence of Saint Sebastian, even if only on canvas, must have kept alive in these rulers the hope that the plague, which had been raging in Lorraine since 1630, would soon end.

There is a replica of this picture in the church of Broglie (Eure) in France. When the original was discovered in Belgium in 1908, it was taken at first to be by Vermeer or some unknown Dutch artist. It was in the Stilwell Collection in New York until it came on to the market in Berlin in 1927. The Matthiesen Gallery presented it to the Berlin Gallery in 1928.

CLAUDE LORRAIN, *c.* 1600–1682
Italian Coastal Landscape. Canvas, 97 × 131 cm. Cat. No. 448 B.
Signed and dated: Claude in. f. Romae 1642.

A shepherd-couple are placed in the foreground of this southern landscape. The woman is seated on a rock and is listening to the shepherd playing the shawm. To the right of the picture is a tent supported by a tree, and on the left a stone bridge leads to a ruined Roman temple. In the background the open sea is half-obscured by the mist of a warm summer's day.

The painter, whose real name was Claude Gellée, was a native of Lorraine. When he first arrived in Rome, he worked as a pastrycook, then as assistant to the landscape-painter Agostino Tassi, whom he helped with decorative work. Not much is known about his early career. It was only in his thirties that he began to acquire stature and reputation as an artist in his own right. The German painter-biographer Joachim von Sandrart, reporting on his visit to Rome (1629–35), writes that Claude was determined 'to become familiar with nature in all its forms, and would spend whole days and late into the night in the fields, so that he learned how to convey most naturally the flush of day, the rising and setting of the sun . . .'.

Characteristic features of Claude's art are the subtle moods of the landscape and the variation in the seascape with the changing seasons. People are unimportant in his pictures; the painter regarded them only as a means of lending animation to his land-scapes and as a rule he did not even paint them himself. In the 1630s he started a book which he gradually filled with pen-and-ink drawings of almost 200 of his own pictures; although it does not comprise his entire œuvre, it is nevertheless a unique documentary record of his artistic creations. The book is preserved today in the British Museum under the title *Liber Veritatis*; in it the Berlin landscape features on p. 64, and according to a note written on the verso, the work was commissioned by a patron in Paris.

This picture is recorded as having been in English private ownership in the early eighteenth century: until 1722 it was in the possession of the Duke of Portland, who sold it to the Earl of Scarbrough. About 1818 it passed into the possession of Count Pourtalès and from him, in 1865, into the collection of the Marquis de la Ganay, from whom Bode bought it in 1881 for the Berlin Gallery.

NICOLAS POUSSIN, 1593–1665
Landscape with St Matthew and the Angel. Canvas, 99 × 135 cm. Cat. No. 478A.

In the Campanian landscape Matthew the Evangelist is sitting on a stone amongst the ruins of ancient buildings, harkening to an angel who stands before him. A painting of St John on Patmos, of similar design and equal size, in the Art Institute of Chicago was originally a companion-piece to the one in Berlin; they probably formed part of an unfinished series of landscapes with the four Evangelists. The two paintings appear to have parted company at an early stage. Unforeseen circumstances seem to have prevented the completion of the series. Cardinal Francesco Barberini, who presumably commissioned Poussin to paint the pictures (this work is mentioned in an inventory of the Palazzo Barberini of 1692), was forced to flee Rome in 1645, following the death of his uncle, Pope Urban VIII; this would have been reason enough for the painter to leave the series unfinished, in which case the St Matthew landscape must have been the only one the Cardinal actually received, and the second picture sold to another buyer. This would suggest that both pictures were painted before or around 1645, this date being borne out by the development of Poussin's style, for he had just returned to Italy after a luckless interlude as Court painter in Paris.

In the Berlin painting Poussin has introduced realistic impressions of nature, deriving ostensibly from the Tiber valley at Aqua Acetosa not far from Rome. But there is no question of an exact reproduction of the topographical features, such as the North European artists in Italy so often tried to achieve. As in all Poussin's works, the composition here is essentially imaginative: the double bend of the river conveys the full depth of the valley, while the soaring tower of a distant ruin is the dominant vertical feature of the landscape, lending emphasis to the quiet dialogue between Evangelist and angel; his own features shaded, Matthew looks up at the divine messenger who stands bathed in a bright light. The remains of the building material, stones cut in cubic and cylindrical forms, not only provide depth and perspective but also lend a note of gravity to this heroic landscape, and are so placed as to achieve the maximum artistic effect.

At the end of the eighteenth century this painting formed part of a legacy to the Colonna di Sciarra family, and its presence in their palazzo was confirmed in 1820. In 1873 it was acquired for the Berlin Gallery.

ANTOINE WATTEAU, 1684–1721
The Dance. Canvas, 97 × 116 cm. On loan from the Federal Republic.

Three children have sat down in the open under a tree to make music. A small girl stands in front of them and seems to pause in the act of dancing. In the distance a village church can be seen. The age of the young dancer seems strangely indeterminate; not yet full grown, she nevertheless gives the impression of being remote from the world of children. As in almost all Watteau's pictures, there is a touch of sadness in this scene. A copper engraving of the painting by C. N. Cochin carries a marginal annotation, which begins with the words: 'Iris c'est de bonne heure avoir l'air à la danse . . .'.

The strangely statuesque quality of the girl, gazing towards the onlooker, recalls the painter's major work *Gilles* in the Louvre in Paris. Both pictures must have been painted in the closing years of the artist's life. Three preliminary sketches by Watteau of the group of seated children have survived (Musée Cognacq-Jay and A. Strölin Collection, Paris; Fogg Art Museum, Cambridge, Mass.). At one time the picture was mounted in a circular frame, traces of this being still visible on the canvas.

Until 1766 this picture formed part of the famous collection of the Amsterdam merchant Gerrit Braamkamp (1699–1771), from whom it may have been purchased on behalf of Frederick II. On the other hand, it is impossible to identify it with certainty among the Watteau paintings known to be in the Prussian palaces in the eighteenth century. In 1876 it was in the Berlin Palace, later in the New Palace in Potsdam. Even after the collapse of the German Empire, the picture remained in the possession of the Hohenzollerns but was later put in the hands of an art-dealer and was purchased in 1942 for the museum which Adolf Hitler had planned for Linz. It returned to Berlin in 1952 on loan from the German Federal Republic.

ANTOINE WATTEAU, 1684–1721
The French Comedy. Canvas, 37 × 48 cm. Cat. No. 468.

In 1734 the *French Comedy* and the *Italian Comedy* (p. 284) were reproduced as copper engravings by C. N. Cochin. He named them respectively 'L'Amour au théâtre français' and 'L'Amour au théâtre italien', thus making the artist's intentions clear.

A shepherd and shepherdess in a park, surrounded by a company of people, form the focal point of the *French Comedy*. Bacchus is reclining on a stone bench, drinking to a huntsman, while musicians provide music for the dance. One must not assume that Watteau had any particular play in mind; he was probably aiming to portray the various characters of the Comedy. This does not mean that he never depicted real people or happenings; at all events he will have taken for granted that the observer or his patron would be able to recognize such details. The gentleman in black on the right is in all probability the well-known actor Paul Poisson.

The theatre plays an important part in Watteau's art. His teacher Gillot, with whom the twenty-year-old Flemish-born painter began his work in Paris, appears to have encouraged this interest in the theatre. Watteau's most famous portrait, the *Gilles* in the Louvre, is the portrayal of a stage character. Stage-play and reality are strangely interwoven, as they are also in his pictures of social occasions, the *fêtes galantes*, which Watteau originated and executed with such artistry. These gained for him recognition by the French Academy.

There is documentary evidence to show that, from 1769 onwards, this painting and its counterpart, the *Italian Comedy*, were in the picture gallery at Sanssouci, having previously formed part of the Henri de Rosnel Collection. The founders of the Berlin Museum, however, steeped as they were in the tradition of Goethe and Winckelmann, had no time for Watteau's art, despising its frivolity. The outstanding collection of the works of French painters that Frederick the Great had built up in Potsdam remained almost untouched when pictures were selected for the Berlin Gallery in 1830. Only two paintings by Watteau, which happened to be the smallest, met with the Commission's approval and were accepted for the Museum: *The French Comedy* and *The Italian Comedy*. *The Enseigne de Gersaint*, at that time only a few steps away in the Berlin Palace, was completely ignored.

JEAN-BAPTISTE-SIMEON CHARDIN, 1699–1779
The Draughtsman. Canvas, 81 × 64 cm. Cat. No. 2076.
Signed and dated 1737.

A young man with a pigtail and a tricorn hat stands at a table sharpening with a knife a crayon in a holder. Before him on a drawing-board lies a half-finished sketch of a bearded man. The same youthful model is to be found in other paintings by Chardin, such as the *House of Cards* in the National Gallery in London and a similar picture in the Oskar Reinhart collection in Winterthur. The individual features of the sitter and the half-length treatment give the picture the character of a portrait, which was not, however, the artist's intention. Chardin's interest lay in the commonplace, in the aesthetic values of everyday life, which he – like Vermeer – brings out in the still-life posture of those he portrayed.

Chardin was received into the Paris Academy in 1728 as an animal and fruit painter. During the 1730s he produced a series of half-length portrayals of children, busily engaged at a table, in the style of *The Draughtsman*. Following the success of the latter, he produced a second version, which – signed and dated 1737 like the Berlin picture – is now in the Louvre. In 1738 *The Draughtsman* – which of the two versions is not certain – was exhibited in the Paris Salon and in 1740 a mezzotint print by J. Faber brought it to the notice of a wider public.

Chardin's work is in striking contrast to the courtly art of his contemporaries, Boucher and Fragonard. In spite of that, or perhaps because of it, he met with considerable success. In a certain sense his pictures represented a bourgeois world, which had grown tired of the cultural domination of the Court. The mere choice of subject satisfied a need for a simpler and more natural life – another component of the age of gallantry – and at the same time, managed to come up to the highest standards of painting.

In 1779 this painting was in Unter den Linden, the Berlin palace of Prince Henry, brother of Frederick II. It may be identical with a picture of Chardin's which the king is known to have bought in 1747 in Paris through Count Rothenburg. The painting, which documentary evidence shows to have been in palaces at Potsdam during the nineteenth century, remained in the possession of the former royal house after the fall of the monarchy and was purchased in 1931 for the Berlin Gallery.

PETER PAUL RUBENS, 1577–1640
The Lamentation. Panel, 34 × 27 cm. Cat. No. 798 K.

The naked body of Christ lies stretched out on a bier, which occupies almost the entire breadth of the panel. Behind the bier the grief-stricken women, the Virgin and Mary Magdalene, stand tearing at their long, flowing hair. Two large torches in the background cast a flickering light over the scene, so that only the figures and the shroud stand out in the darkness of the room.

The painter treated the theme of the Lamentation on several occasions. In Rubens' development of the subject, however, the Berlin sketch stands alone in that it was never followed up or even completed. The powerful effect produced by the three figures placed at right angles and reinforced by the uncannily empty areas of darkness might have been difficult to achieve in a larger format; the sketch bears all the signs of being a first idea. The modelling of the male body, the subtle use of shadow in the white cloth and not least the blonde tresses (rendered with a wide brush) which envelop the faces of the weeping women, all reveal the masterly assurance of the great Flemish artist.

The women's violent gestures, the dramatic light-effect and the realism of the naked body were undoubtedly inspired by impressions gained while Rubens was in Italy, and in particular in Rome by the art of Caravaggio. We know that, during the years he spent in the south, the painter became preoccupied with the Lamentation as a theme. It is, therefore, not unreasonable to count this sketch among the works he produced in Italy, particularly as it was purchased from an Italian collection. Equally, however, the colours and brushwork of the small *Lamentation* suggest that, despite Rubens' southern memories, it may have been painted shortly after his return to Antwerp in 1609. That he continued for a long time to draw on the artistic experience he had gained in Italy is shown by the pictures he subsequently painted, among them the *Saint Sebastian* (p. 213).

Nothing is known of the provenance of this picture before it was bought for the Berlin Gallery in 1880 from the Demidoff Collection in Florence.

PETER PAUL RUBENS, 1577–1640
Saint Sebastian. Canvas, 200 × 120 cm. Cat. No. 798H.

After Sebastian had survived execution by bowmen and protested publicly against the persecution of the Christians, the Roman Emperor had him slain. The miraculous deliverance of the saint, transfixed by arrows, was regarded even in early times as a parallel to the resurrection of Christ. The figure of the martyr as portrayed by Rubens is also intended to recall the Crucifixion. Bound to a tree, his eyes turned upwards to heaven, he seems only slightly affected by the bleeding wounds. The way in which the bound man twists his body may be taken as a sign of pain but this does not lessen its beauty, which is that of a hero of antiquity.

In his Sebastian picture, which must have been painted *c.* 1614, Rubens realized many of the impressions he had gained during his eight years in Italy (1600–08). The sculptural, corporeal quality of the saint's figure reminds one both of the antique and of Michelangelo's works. The contrasting light and shade and the realistic treatment of detail were touches that Rubens had learned from Caravaggio. But in combining the statuesque figure with the atmosphere of an evening landscape, the Flemish painter surpassed his Roman master. Here the tragedy of the event finds adequate expression in the language of nature.

In a letter of 1618 to Sir Dudley Carlton, Rubens mentions a selection of his own paintings, which he had kept back in his house 'for his own pleasure' and which he was prepared to exchange for works of art in the possession of the English diplomat. Among the pictures included in the painter's offer is a 'naked Saint Sebastian by my hand', in all probability the one now in Berlin. Subsequently all trace of it is lost and it comes to light again only in the nineteenth century (Hill auction, London 1811; Munro auction, London 1878). In 1879 the painting was purchased for the Berlin Gallery.

PETER PAUL RUBENS, 1577–1640
The Child with a Bird. Panel, 49 × 40 cm. Cat. No. 763.

A child of about two is shown playing with a captive bird. On the original panel, which was smaller, only the child's head was visible. Rubens made use of this study for an angel in the *Madonna with a floral wreath* in the Munich Pinakothek. But we also find the head again on the exterior of the Stephanus Altar at Valenciennes. Later the artist enlarged the picture on the left side, adding the hands with the bird.

Although formerly taken to be a girl, the child portrayed is in all probability Rubens' first son Albert, who was born in 1614. The same child, though seen full-face, is to be found in a red-chalk drawing by Rubens in the Hermitage in Leningrad. It was a common practice for relations of the artist to be employed as models in commissioned works. A pen-and-ink drawing in the British Museum showing Cupid and Psyche carries an instruction, which was perhaps intended for the artist's assistants, that his small son Albert should be employed as a model for the Cupid ('Cupido, ex Albertuli mei imagine'). Sir Anthony van Dyck, the painter's outstanding pupil, was working in Rubens' atelier when the Berlin picture was painted. It was at one time suggested that it was he who painted the picture but this assumption cannot be supported on stylistic evidence.

The motif of the child playing with a bird goes back to antiquity. It also crops up frequently in Christian art. The bird symbolizes the soul or life, which passes all too quickly. In many pictures of the Virgin and Child, Jesus is portrayed holding a bird in his hand as an allusion to his death and resurrection. Whether Rubens had a similar allegory in mind when he introduced the bird into his child-portrait, or whether some particular incident in his own life motivated him, is not known. Children, who were at that time closer to death than they are today, played an important part in Rubens' life and work. His *Perseus and Andromeda* (p. 217) is an eloquent example of the artist's epic genius for introducing children directly into the action portrayed.

This picture, which had been in the royal palaces since the eighteenth century, was transferred to the Berlin Gallery in 1830.

214

PETER PAUL RUBENS, 1577–1640
Perseus and Andromeda. Panel, 99 × 137 cm. Cat. No. 785.

Chained to a rock, Andromeda, daughter of the King of Ethiopia, was to be sacrificed to a sea-monster. The king had been ordered to make this sacrifice, in order to make amends for the arrogance of his wife, Cassiopeia. As Perseus, who had vanquished the dreaded Gorgon Medusa, was returning home on his winged horse, Pegasus, he caught sight of the chained Andromeda and delivered her from the threat of the monster. Overcome by the beauty of the young princess, her liberator confessed his love: 'Oh, thou deservest not chains such as these but only the bonds that unite passionate lovers' (Ovid).

Rubens knew how to translate the popular, widely-known poetry of Ovid into his own special language. On a sea-girt spur of rock Perseus steps towards the royal princess. Dressed in gleaming armour and in the red cloak of the conqueror, he loosens the chains binding the naked maiden, who stands with downcast eyes. Two putti, who, to the best of their ability, are lending a hand, also seem not uninterested in the human side of the encounter; three others are attending to the winged, dapple-grey horse, which is impatiently pawing the rock with its hoof. In the depths of the blue sea the winding coils of the monster appear.

Rubens treated the same theme in a picture of similar size and design, now in the Hermitage in Leningrad. It shows Perseus at the centre of the action and was clearly the forerunner of the Berlin painting. Only in the latter did the painter find full freedom of expression and the correct proportions for the relief-type composition.

Many pictorial themes in Flemish Baroque painting, particularly that of the humanist and diplomat Rubens, are by no means confined to depicting events. The story of Andromeda, for example, was also given political significance, and this kind of material, as an allegory of oppression and liberation in the struggle against enemy powers, was open to a great variety of interpretations. Indeed, the Berlin picture was painted at practically the same time as Rubens' most important work in the field of political allegory, the great cycle of wall-paintings commissioned by Marie de Médicis in Paris in 1622.

The *Perseus and Andromeda* was in the Pasquier Collection before being auctioned in Paris in 1755. Records show that from 1764 it was in the picture gallery at Sanssouci until it was transferred to the Berlin Museum in 1830.

PETER PAUL RUBENS, 1577–1640
Landscape with Cows and Wildfowlers. Panel, 113 × 176 cm. Cat. No. 2013.

On the edge of a wood, through which flows a stream, stands a herd of cattle. The last rays of the evening sun are shining through the trees, bathing the landscape in warm light. As maids from the nearby farm milk the cows, a wildfowler fires at a duck. The great variety of tree-trunks and foliage, of plants and animals, typifies that natural scheme of things in which air and water, light and warmth, sunshine and rain are provided in accordance with God's plan. That a peaceful life and the threat of death are never far apart is demonstrated by the disturbing proximity of the fowler with his gun to the women at work.

Of the large and varied number of pictures Rubens completed in his lifetime, relatively few were landscapes, and of these the Berlin painting is one of the few in large format; it has a close affinity with two others, one of which is in the Royal Collection in London, the other in the Munich Pinakothek. Several of the figures in all three pictures are alike, although they are disposed in different ways. This does not detract from the significance of each individual work, but it does throw an interesting light on the painter's methods of working and on his habit of referring back to earlier sketches and studies. To judge by its composition and style of painting, the Berlin picture was the last of the group and must have been painted around 1630. In designing the forest, Rubens broke away almost entirely from previous sketches and with surprising artistic licence developed a quite novel arrangement of light and shade. The steep angle of the sun's rays creates a remarkable feeling of space and atmosphere. The lively brushwork gives an impression of complete spontaneity on the part of the artist, who was in no way inhibited by having to make corrections and may even have allowed for an extension of the panel-format.

This painting was in the Duc de Richelieu's collection in the seventeenth century, together with two other Rubens works now in the Berlin Gallery, *Andromeda chained to the Rock* and *The Shipwreck of Aeneas* (p. 285). In a description of the collector's art-treasures by Roger de Piles, published in 1677, this landscape is entitled *Les Vaches.* The Duke, a great-nephew of the famous Cardinal of the same name, took the opportunity, while on Louis XIV's campaigns in the Netherlands, to buy important works by Rubens. In the eighteenth century the picture travelled to England, when it came into the possession of Sir William Lowther; later it entered the Earl of Burlington's collection of paintings at Holker Hall, Lancashire. In 1857 it was on public display at the famous exhibition in Manchester; eleven years later it was acquired by the Duke of Devonshire. It was bought for the Berlin Gallery in 1927.

PETER PAUL RUBENS, 1577–1640
Saint Cecilia. Panel, 177 × 139 cm. Cat. No. 781.

In this composition, the only large-scale work on this subject by Rubens, he portrays the saint, who is revered as the patron of music, playing a spinet at the foot of a formal, architectural vista of pillars. Beyond the terrace-like room stretches an expanse of Flemish landscape, yet the presence of the angels emphasizes the sublime character of the scene. As her fingers touch the keys of her instrument, the saint is entranced by celestial music and in her face is reflected the heavenly paradise towards which she gazes, wide-eyed.

The Berlin *Saint Cecilia* is one of the last pictures which Rubens painted, apart from official commissions towards the end of his life. As in so many pictures during this later period, Hélène Fourment, who had become his second wife in 1630, served as the artist's model. The bold and rapid application of colour is vivacious and rich in delicate nuances: deep emerald green appears side by side with dark red and brilliant yellow, emphasizing the pale, enamel-like flesh-tones. There are many corrections to the painted surface which show that Rubens altered considerable portions of the picture while working on it, and even enlarged the panel on the left-hand side.

The formal interpretation in the composition in no way detracts from the human, almost intimate, touches which Rubens has employed in depicting the saint. The casually worn cloak, the foot withdrawn from the shoe, the sleeping dog, and, last but not least, the features of Hélène Fourment are all products of highly personal experience. The painter transforms the youthful body of his model into a monumental figure which combines, in a most moving way, portrait and sacred image.

This painting, which was found in Rubens' house following his death (1640), was presented the following year by his family to Jakob van Ophem in Brussels as a token of their gratitude for the help he had given in administering the artist's estate. Later it found its way to Paris, where the young Watteau saw it and made a crayon drawing of it. In 1742 the picture passed from the Prince de Carignan to the Duc de Tallard, from whom Frederick the Great bought it in 1756 for his gallery at Sanssouci. From there it was transferred in 1830 to the Berlin Museum.

ADRIAEN BROUWER, c. 1605–1638
Dune Landscape by Moonlight. Panel, 25 × 34 cm. Cat. No. 853B.
Signed with the monogram AB

Beyond the dunes rising towards the right, and the silhouette of a village church, stretches a vista of brightly moonlit sea. Ragged clouds scudding across the sky create a patchwork of light and dark over the scene, in which the hut to the right stands out eerily. In the foreground three peasants are deep in conversation.

Adriaen Brouwer worked in Frans Hals' studio in Haarlem around 1625 and, although the two artists had widely divergent interests, this association considerably influenced Brouwer's style and continued to do so for the rest of his life. In 1631 he returned to his Flemish homeland and the following year he became a member of the Painters' Guild in Antwerp, where he remained until his early death in 1638. Brouwer's unconventional way of life provided his biographers with a wealth of material and he has acquired something of a legendary reputation as a gifted bohemian.

Although Brouwer based most of his works on the world of peasants and artisans, few of them take the form of landscapes. These were all painted in the closing years of his life and are among the treasures of Flemish art. If the Berlin Gallery has three of them, it has Wilhelm Bode in particular to thank for this, for he wrote a definitive study (1884) which led to the rediscovery of this painter. All the same, Brouwer's paintings were greatly admired, collected and copied during his lifetime. Among those who rated them highly was Rubens, and this landscape may well be one of the sixteen pictures by Brouwer that were in Rubens' possession, for the inventory made after his death includes 'a landscape by moonlight'. With their sweeping, fluent brushwork and the delicate gradations of colour on a brown ground, they do in fact closely resemble the late landscapes of Rubens, although they radiate a quite different atmosphere.

The provenance of the Berlin painting can be traced only as far as the nineteenth century. Prior to 1870 it was in the Brentano Collection in Frankfurt on Main; it then came into the possession of Barthold Suermondt, to reach Berlin in 1874 when his collection was acquired by the Museum.

Sir Anthony van Dyck, 1599–1641
Portrait of a Genoese Lady. Canvas, 200 × 116 cm. Cat. No. 782 C.

The lady, relaxed yet dignified, wears the elegant black costume of Italian society, a style of dress inspired by the formal attire of the Spanish Court. The white lace ruff, which shows off the face to such advantage, and the frilled sleeves are the most striking decorative features of the dress. On her slender hands, resting lightly on the arms of the chair, the lady wears no ring; in her right she holds a fan. A piece of fine lace, a so-called 'peak', which hangs down from the hair-line almost to the bridge of the nose, graces the lady's high forehead. A deep-red carpet provides an effective contrast to the other sombre tones. As a background the artist has included a dark curtain and the outline of a column and its massive base.

Van Dyck entered the Antwerp workshop of Rubens at an early age, and in due course became his outstanding pupil and assistant. Though he began by adhering closely to the style of his teacher, so considerable was his talent that, under the influence of Italian art, and particularly of Venetian painting, he developed his own distinctive style while still in his twenties. He spent several years in Genoa (1622–27), gaining both recognition and important commissions from members of noble families, who sought above all to have their portraits painted by him. He satisfied their need for self-projection in fastidious full-length portraits of the kind established by Titian as the accepted Court style. This portrait shared a common history with a male companion-piece (p. 285); these twin portraits in the Berlin Gallery belong to the Genoese period, but no one has so far been able to identify the subjects.

The first mention of the two pictures in a description of 1773, where their location is given as the Palazzo Giacomo Balbi in Genoa. The artist David Wilkie saw the paintings in 1827 in the Palazzo Spinola and recommended them to Sir Robert Peel, who purchased them for his collection the following year. In 1829 they were publicly exhibited in London at the British Institution. A view of the exhibition-hall painted by Scarlett Davis shows the portraits among other works by Netherlandish masters. The two pictures were purchased for Berlin when paintings from Sir Robert Peel's collection were put up for auction in London in 1900.

VELAZQUEZ, 1599–1660
Portrait of Countess Olivares. Canvas, 120 × 99 cm. Cat. No. 413E.

In this three-quarter length portrait the sitter is shown dressed for some ceremonial occasion; her right hand rests on the back of a chair, and in her face there is the hint of a smile. Her jewellery is unusually lavish: she wears a diamond rose in her hair and pearl ear-rings, and over her richly patterned dress hangs a heavy gold chain. The sleeves are decorated with gold brocade and edged with gold lace. In her hand, on which she is wearing costly rings, she holds a fan.

The back of the canvas is said formerly to have carried the inscription 'Joana de Miranda', the name of the painter's wife. We do not know with any certainty what Velázquez' wife looked like; on the other hand, it is well known that in the case of portraits by a famous artist in which the sitter could not be identified, legends tended to develop around some member or other of his family. The exquisite dress and the courtly bearing of the lady rather suggest someone attached to the court of Philip IV, where the name Miranda was not unfamiliar. A drawing in the Albertina in Vienna and a copper-engraving of 1627 have lent support to the view that the subject of the portrait was the wife of the Conde de Olivares; her full name was Dona Inés de Zúñiga, Condesa de Olivares, Duquesa de San-Lúcar.

Velázquez, who came from Seville, went to Madrid at the age of twenty-two, where he gained recognition so quickly that within two years he was appointed Court painter to Philip IV. He later became a gentleman-in-waiting and chamberlain and throughout his life maintained his close relations with the royal family.

The number of female portraits which Velázquez painted is very small, particularly if one excludes the official portraits of royal consorts. This may be due to the social status of women in Spain, which was quite different from that in a country like Italy. This difference may also explain the air of distinguished aloofness which radiates from the Berlin painting.

At one time in the Sebastian Martinez Collection in Cadiz, the portrait was purchased by the Earl of Dudley from the Salamanca Gallery in 1867; twenty years later it passed into the possession of the Berlin Museum.

FRANS HALS, *c.* 1580–1666
Nurse with a Child. Canvas, 86 × 65 cm. Cat. No. 801G.

The somewhat inappropriate title was probably given to this picture when it was put on the market in 1872. The contrast between the expensively clad child and the soberly dressed woman could be explained by attributing to the latter the inferior social position of nurse. But she is wearing the sort of black dress typical among bourgeois women of the period which can be observed in other Dutch portraits. There is, therefore, no reason to see the woman other than as the mother of the child. The child is undoubtedly the main figure in the picture, a fact which is literally underlined by the dress, which is of Italian brocade; it is further embellished with a ruby locket. As it was the custom not to differentiate between the sexes in dressing young children, it is impossible to be sure whether this is a boy or a girl.

Frans Hals was born in Antwerp between 1581 and 1585. While he was still young, his parents emigrated to Haarlem, where, after serving his apprenticeship with Carel van Mander, he became a member of the painters' guild in 1610. The artist's early years are still shrouded in mystery. We have no reliable information on what work the painter was doing up to his thirtieth year. As a result, the paintings he produced in the fourth decade of his life have come to be regarded as early works, in which category this portrait, which was painted *c.* 1620, also belongs. In fact, the painstaking detail evident in the costume, particularly the lace-trimmings and the brocade pattern, is very much in the tradition of the older portrait-painters. On the other hand, there is a freshness in the composition and a delicacy in the use of light that places Frans Hals apart from his predecessors. Facing the onlooker, the woman responds with a smile to the child's outstretched arm. The fruit in her hand affirms the silent dialogue in a way that only Frans Hals in his most sensitive mood could portray.

In 1872 this picture, which had been in Ilpenstein Castle, was auctioned with the contents of the castle in Amsterdam. It is not known how long it had been there or whether there was any family connection between the sitter and the Tedding van Berkhout family, who had occupied the castle. In 1874 the painting was acquired, with the Suermondt Collection, by the Berlin Gallery.

FRANS HALS, c. 1580–1666
Malle Babbe. Canvas, 75 × 64 cm. Cat. No. 801 C.

The back of the picture carries an old inscription, which reads 'Malle Babbe van Haarlem p. Frans Hals'. The old woman with the owl on her shoulder and the jug of wine in front of her has stirred the imagination of admirers of this work to all kinds of fictional interpretations, which range from a witch to a sailor's wench and which, for the most part, draw their inspiration from the bohemian world. But this type of artistic romanticism must have been just as alien to Frans Hals as the allegorical picture of his day is to the modern observer. The attributes of Malle Babbe are the only pointers to the hidden meaning of the picture. The owl, regarded from ancient times as a symbol of wisdom, was also regarded as a bird that prefers darkness to light. Allied to the demons of the night, it could represent madness or drunkenness, and to this day the owl retains similar associations.

The Dutch painter Louis Bernhard Coclers made an etching of Malle Babbe which has affinities with the Berlin picture. Copies were widely distributed in the eighteenth century, accompanied by a verse which, freely translated, runs: 'You think your owl's a falcon, O Babel, that's well done. Play on with your illusion. You're not the only one!' These words of wisdom are aimed at those people who cannot live without illusions, fortified if necessary with the help of wine.

We do not know who the woman was whom Frans Hals employed as a model in this and other pictures. Jan Steen appears to have owned one of them, which has since disappeared, for it can be recognized in the background of *The Christening* (p. 289); here it is shown hanging above a table, around which a group of drinkers are gathered, together with a male companion-piece now in the Cassel Museum. This latter work shows a popular stage-character, 'Pickelhering', a bibulous joker who was a regular feature of contemporary comedies.

The earliest documentary record of this painting occurs when it was auctioned in Amsterdam in 1834. In 1869 it was placed on public exhibition in Munich. Gustave Courbet copied it at that time – his picture is in the Hamburg Kunsthalle – and he was not the only artist of the period to see in Frans Hals his spiritual forbear, whose free style of painting seemed to anticipate Impressionism. In 1874 the picture was acquired for Berlin with the rest of the Suermondt Collection.

REMBRANDT HARMENSZ VAN RIJN, 1606–1669
Landscape with a Bridge. Panel, 28 × 40 cm. Cat. No. 1932.

A rough road in the right foreground draws the observer's eye to some houses on the outskirts of a village. A wooden footbridge crosses the stream by the roadside and leads to a hill, which is partly covered with clumps of trees and which forms the centre-piece of the composition. On the left is a flat landscape, traversed by a river; a stone bridge, the several arches of which are reflected in the water, is the most striking feature of the middle ground.

In the wide range of Rembrandt's œuvre there are relatively few landscapes. From the mid-1630s onwards he painted a series of imaginary landscapes, all of them imbued with a certain expressive quality; there is too a gloomy, almost uncanny air about this example. Storm clouds have darkened the sky and only the clumps of trees on the hill are caught by pale rays of sunshine. The marked contrast of light and shade heightens all the physical features, yet almost the only colours used are shades of brown-green; the few natural colours have little bearing on the overall effect.

The style of painting and the range of colours employed here recall the rare pictures of the painter and etcher Hercules Seghers, who around the mid-1630s settled in Amsterdam and may well have aroused Rembrandt's interest in landscape-painting. That Rembrandt admired his art is proved by the fact that he himself owned several of Seghers' works. Two of this artist's landscapes can be seen in the Berlin Gallery; compared with these, Rembrandt's works are more deeply imbued with Baroque expression. The Berlin landscape carries no date, but to judge by its style it must have been painted at the end of the 1630s.

The painting was acquired for the gallery of the Grand Duke of Oldenburg in 1801, and was purchased in 1924 for the Berlin Museum.

REMBRANDT HARMENSZ VAN RIJN, 1606–1669
The Mennonite Preacher Anslo. Canvas, 176 × 210 cm. Cat. No. 828L.
Signed and dated: Rembrandt f. 1641

Cornelis Claesz Anslo (1592–1646) was the head of the Mennonite community in Amsterdam and a well-known preacher. This painting, which is dated 1641, shows him in his study with an open Bible before him, giving spiritual instruction to a woman. The eloquent gesture of his left hand is so spontaneous that it seems almost to project from the canvas. The posture of the woman, whose hands are resting quietly in her lap, reflects her absorption as she listens to his words. She has been taken at various times to be the wife or the mother of the preacher, but this has never been substantiated. Rembrandt probably painted the picture for an old people's home which Anslo's father had founded. It is even possible that the woman portrayed lived in this home.

Holland's greatest poet of the seventeenth century, Joost van den Vondel, wrote a quatrain in which he made fun of Rembrandt's efforts to portray Anslo: 'Oh, Rembrandt, paint Cornelis' voice/the visible is the least in him/the invisible one knows only through the ears/anyone wishing to see Anslo must hear him'. Vondel's lines allude to a matter of theological dispute, in which the Protestants claimed that the word was essentially superior to the image; thus the man could only be portrayed in terms of his soul and of his works, not in his physical being. Rembrandt also captured Anslo's features in two drawings and an etching, which clearly preceded the Berlin painting, but it was in the latter that the preacher's eloquence became a theme in itself, turning a mere portrait into a scene. It is quite likely that this compelling composition was, in the first instance, a reply to the poet's challenge to make Anslo's voice visible.

The portrait was in the Earl of Ashburnham's collection, from which Wilhelm Bode acquired it in 1894 for the Berlin Gallery. Bode mentions the purchase in his memoirs and the simultaneous acquisition of the *Portrait of a Young Lady in Profile* (p. 145) attributed to Domenico Veneziano. There are records of Rembrandt's portrait in The Hague in 1766 (Aldewereld auction) and, from 1794, in England (Sir Thomas Dundas).

REMBRANDT HARMENSZ VAN RIJN, 1606–1669
Susannah and the Elders. Panel, 76 × 91 cm. Cat. No. 828 E.
Signed and dated: Rembrandt f. 1647

The story of the beautiful Susannah, which is told in the Apocryphal section of the
Book of Daniel, is an allegory of wifely virtue which was one of the favourite themes
of European painters. Susannah, the wife of an eminent man in Babylon, is spied upon
by two men while she is bathing in her garden. They are the most senior judges of the
town, who demand to have their will of her, otherwise they will testify to having found
Susannah with a lover. The defenceless woman refuses to yield to the threat: 'For if I
do this thing, it is death unto me: and if I do it not, I cannot escape your hands. It is
better for me to fall into your hands, and not do it, than to sin in the sight of the Lord.'
As Susannah refuses to give way to the judges, she is accused of adultery and found
guilty. Only at the very last moment does she escape the death-sentence. The young
Daniel succeeds in discrediting the testimony of the two Elders and they are duly
punished.

Rembrandt portrays the scene at its dramatic climax. Susannah has heard the threaten-
ing voice behind her and, faced with an agonizing choice between temporal and ever-
lasting death, her eyes seem to implore the onlooker for help. Only her naked body
and her exquisite red cloak are bathed in bright light. The crowded scene on the right
half of the picture contrasts with the 'void' of darkness on the left. The boldness of the
unbalanced composition is made fully apparent by the use of light.

Rembrandt's composition was presumably inspired by a similar picture by his
teacher Pieter Lastman (p. 288). A drawing of Lastman's *Susannah* and further studies
by Rembrandt for this painting are in the Berlin Kupferstichkabinett (engravings
section). They provide a rare insight into the painter's method of working and indicate
a long and complicated process of gestation which goes back as far as the 1630s. Rembrandt himself altered the picture several times before he finally completed it in 1647,
the date inscribed beside his signature.

The painting, of which there is a record in Amsterdam in 1738 (Schoenborn Collection), travelled to England in the eighteenth century and was in the possession of
the painter Sir Joshua Reynolds. Bode acquired it in 1883 for Berlin from the Lechmere
Collection.

REMBRANDT HARMENSZ VAN RIJN, 1606–1669
Man in a Golden Helmet. Canvas, 67 × 50 cm. Cat. No. 811A.

Rembrandt's portrait was particularly admired by the generation of Impressionist painters as a model example of their own view of art. It has lost none of its popularity, despite commercial exploitation, although it is questionable whether this has contributed to a genuine appreciation of the picture. All too many reproductions have given the public a preconceived image of it, before actually seeing the original. It is therefore all the more necessary to try to make a detached assessment of the work.

Bode regarded the helmet, 'which, in the full sunlight which falls on it, glows and glitters like a heap of precious stones', as primarily an artistic end in itself. Bode's generation, too, may have viewed the work in a more sentimental light, associating it with knights of yore and deeds of heroism. It was precisely these associations that prompted attempts to rob the unknown man with the sinister expression of his anonymity and to link him with the personal life of the painter; the theory that the man was Rembrandt's brother, Adriaen, a cobbler in Leyden, has never been substantiated.

The painting, which dates from *c.* 1650, is not a portrait in the strictest sense; it was not commissioned, as so many portraits were, by prosperous Dutch citizens. The artist has captured not the splendidly armoured figure of an officer or general of his time but the tired features of an old man, who occasionally sat for him, and the gleaming splendour of an old helmet, which was part of Rembrandt's collection.

The painter's tendency to change the normal appearance of people – himself not excluded – by the use of finery and costumes is noticeable in a number of his pictures. Nevertheless, one cannot afford to neglect the motives which first inspired the artist to choose his theme, even if it offers little scope for original interpretation. Was it Rembrandt's intention to portray the unknown man as Mars? The God of War, richly helmeted, is by no means unknown as a theme in Dutch painting. The fact that such questions of interpretation are posed at all is characteristic of Rembrandt's art, in which the material and the spiritual are indissolubly linked.

The recorded history of this painting is limited to just over a hundred years. Bode bought it in 1897 from a London art-dealer for the Kaiser-Friedrich Museum Society, which he had founded the year before to support the Picture Gallery and the Collection of Sculptures.

REMBRANDT HARMENSZ VAN RIJN, 1606–1669
Christ and the Samaritan Woman at the Well. Panel, 46·5 × 39 cm. Cat. No. 811 B.
Signed and dated: Rembrandt f. 1659

In the fourth chapter of the Gospel of St John the story is told how Jesus, on his way to Galilee, rested by a well. He asked a woman from Samaria, who was drawing water, for a drink. In the dialogue that followed Jesus spoke symbolically of the living water of God: 'Whosoever drinketh of this water shall thirst again; but whosoever drinketh of the water that I shall give him shall never thirst.'

As so often in Rembrandt's work, there is a surprising quality of wilfulness in his treatment of the subject. In the centre of the composition stands the Samaritan woman, drawing the bucket of water from the well. Her eyes are fixed on Christ, who stands – completely in shadow – at the right-hand edge of the picture. Behind the well one can see the head of a child. Bright light falls only on the buildings in the background, whereas the encounter itself takes place in quiet half-shadow, while on the left several disciples can be seen approaching.

Rembrandt used this same theme on several occasions, sometimes in graphic form. A preliminary sketch for this picture is now in Oxford. A painting on the same theme, attributed to Giorgione, was in the artist's house, but it is no longer possible to identify the work. One is tempted to assume that it was not without influence on Rembrandt when he came to tackle the biblical story. There are certainly clear traces of Venetian influence in his Berlin picture. The bold, impasto-style application of colour in this relatively small panel are reminiscent of a sketch, but no finished painting with a similar composition seems ever to have existed.

Beside the signature the Berlin picture bears the date 1659, which means that it was painted in the same year as the imposing *Moses* (p. 243). These two works have in common a range of colours based largely on tones of brown and an impressionistic style of brushwork. The small panel, on the other hand, has certain distinguishing features, in particular the rich red in the Samaritan woman's cloak.

The picture is known to have been in several different collections since the eighteenth century (I. Blackwood 1778; Van Mulden, Brussels; Lewis Fry, Bristol; Ch. Sedelmeyer, Paris). Finally it was part of the Rudolf Kann collection in Paris, where Bode bought it in 1907 for the Gallery.

Rembrandt Harmensz van Rijn, 1606–1669
Moses holds aloft the Tables of the Law. Canvas, 167 × 135 cm. Cat. No. 811.
Signed and dated: Rembrandt, f. 1659

When Moses came down from Mount Sinai to bring his people the Tables of the Law which he had received from God, he found the Israelites dancing round the golden calf; they were making a thank-offering to the golden image for their deliverance from slavery in Egypt. 'And it came to pass, as soon as he came nigh unto the camp, that he saw the calf, and the dancing: and Moses' anger waxed hot, and he cast the tables out of his hands, and brake them beneath the mount.' (Exodus xxxii, 19.)

The solitary figure of the prophet stands, bathed in a supernatural radiance, against a rocky background with a ruddy expanse of sky beyond. His face, of which the Bible said that it shone because he had talked with God, is the focal point of the picture and is framed in a rhomboid formed by the arms holding aloft the tablets. On the nearer of the two are written in Hebrew the first five commandments.

The detached calm of the picture has raised repeated doubts as to whether Rembrandt in fact set out to portray the prophet's anger rather than the act of displaying the new Tables of the Law. It is difficult to avoid the conclusion, however, that the painter's aim was to present the moment of destruction. The marked emphasis laid on the single, imposing figure and the deliberate absence of any dramatic elements is entirely in keeping with Rembrandt's style of composition during his later period and with his tendency to sublimate biblical material.

Rembrandt's *Moses* was painted in 1659, possibly together with another of his paintings in the Berlin Gallery, which is also a life-size portrayal from the Old Testament. This, a smaller picture, though apparently cut down in size, is *Jacob wrestling with the Angel* (p. 289) and, to judge by the style, it must have been painted at about the same time. The contention that the Moses picture was originally intended for the town-hall in Amsterdam but was later withdrawn by the artist does not carry much conviction. The mere fact that the painting has retained its original dimensions and was completed without any major interruption argues against such a hypothesis.

During the eighteenth century and prior to its transfer to the Berlin Gallery in 1834, this painting was in the possession of the Kings of Prussia. It is recorded for the first time in the catalogue of the picture gallery at Sanssouci, published in 1764. The compiler of the catalogue, Matthias Österreich, recommends the visitor to view the picture from a certain distance, 'as one can then admire the great freedom with which it is painted'.

REMBRANDT HARMENSZ VAN RIJN, 1606–1669
Portrait of Henrickje Stoffels. Canvas, 86 × 65 cm. Cat. No. 828 B.

Hendrickje Stoffels (*c.* 1625–63) lived in Rembrandt's house from about 1645. She became his second wife, although the relationship could never be legalized. Presumably their marriage was prevented by the conditions of the will of his first wife Saskia who died in 1642. Owing to the irregular nature of this second marriage, Rembrandt was forbidden for a time to take communion. Following his financial failure in 1656, when his entire possessions were put up for auction, Hendrickje together with Titus, Rembrandt's son by the first marriage, started their own art-dealing business, and to protect him from his creditors, the painter was registered as an employee in the family business.

The Berlin painting, which was produced during a period of severe personal stress in the late 1650s, is the finest extant portrait of Hendrickje. In a relaxed pose, the young woman gazes straight out from the canvas, her hands resting in the opening of a stable-type door, as if she had just emerged from the darkness of the house. The optical fusion of the painted door-frame with the picture's real frame virtually cancels out the effect of distance between them. Despite the structural balance of the composition the impression of spontaneity remains; the artist observes how the cord around Hendrickje's neck drops to one side as she makes a casual movement. Rembrandt must have attached just as much significance to the simple neck-cord, to which a ring or a key is attached, as to the pearl bracelet, for ring and key were regarded as symbols of marital and wifely virtue.

The colour in this painting is applied with broad strokes in the manner of impasto. The folds of the dress emerge from the dark ground in a blaze of white, golden yellow and deep red. Bright sunlight brings the flesh-colour to life. The deep, warm, glowing colours are characteristic of Rembrandt's later style after the 1650s.

The portrait was in various English collections during the nineteenth century (T. G. Graham White Auction 1878; John Wardell Auction 1879). When Bode acquired it in 1879 – it was his first purchase of a Rembrandt for Berlin – no one was prepared to accept the attribution to the master. This is symptomatic of the unhappy state of Rembrandt research at that time, before Bode began to lay the foundations for it.

JACOB VAN RUISDAEL, 1628–1682
Oak Wood by a Lake with Water-lilies. Canvas, 114 × 141 cm. Cat. No. 885G.
Signed: J. v. Ruisdael

A dense clump of mature oak-trees, over which heavy clouds are gathering, stands on the shore of a lake, providing a dark background for a dead tree-trunk which is caught in the pale sunlight. Its contorted shape is mirrored in the black, marshy water, and its branches stretch out like ghostly arms. The motif of the dead tree, which is condemned to decay, is a reminder that all life is transitory and reflects a melancholy trait which runs through all the artist's work. The dark surface of the water, which takes up the entire foreground of the picture, suggests a landscape devoid of human life, but a shepherd with his flock can be seen passing through the wood. Otherwise, there is no sign, even in the distance, of human life, of a house or a boat.

Goethe was the first to recognize the element of poetry in Ruisdael's work and admired his 'complete symbolism', yet sentimental, romantic thoughts are very far from his mind when he described the dead tree which he saw in Ruisdael's *Landscape with Monastery* in the Dresden Gallery. There the leafless beech-tree reminds him rather of the inevitability of growth and decay: 'Lest its splendidly portrayed trunk should sadden rather than gladden our hearts, it is accompanied by other trees, still in the fullness of life, which by the richness of their branches and twigs come to the aid of the bare trunk.' Goethe's impressions seem more matter-of-fact than those of a modern observer, who is more likely to appreciate the artist's intentions now that the symbolic roots of Dutch painting are better understood.

Jacob van Ruisdael, like his uncle, the painter Salomon van Ruysdael, came from Haarlem. He settled in Amsterdam *c.* 1656 and remained there until his death in 1682. The *Oak Wood* was completed during his early years in Amsterdam and is one of a group of works that show the same impressive composition and a certain Baroque feeling. A wooded landscape in the Hermitage at Leningrad bears a close similarity to the Berlin picture and, though of smaller dimensions, represents a further development of the same theme.

Formerly in the possession of a private collector in England in the nineteenth century (William Wells collection, Redleaf), the painting was exhibited in London at the British Institution in 1848, and in Manchester in 1857. Bode acquired it in 1891 from a Paris art-dealer.

ADRIAEN VAN DE VELDE, 1636–1672
The Farm. Canvas, 63 × 78 cm. Cat. No. 922 C.
Signed and dated: A. v. Velde f. 1666

Unlike the works of the Dutch painters of previous generations, and unlike Ruisdael's rather melancholy portrayal of nature, van de Velde's landscapes are always polished, clean and tidy. Even the animals have their appointed place. While he was still young, van de Velde, obviously under the influence of the painter Paulus Potter, took up the study of animals. Later on he introduced them into other painters' works as accessories. It was in keeping with the general development of Dutch art that interest in the elemental and the heroic as a theme for pictorial art steadily lost ground to bourgeois well-being, which gave rise to Friedländer's apt remark that Dutch artists of the later generation, whatever specialized field they had embarked upon, had one thing in common: an aversion for wind and rough weather.

Van de Velde shows a remarkable talent for portraying natural growth in any form. Without apparent effort, he presents a vast variety of trees and foliage without ever losing sight of the whole. In his pictures man and animal are closely linked with nature, and the clarity of design, the freshness of the colours and, in most cases, the brightness of the sky create a tranquil, holiday atmosphere. Bode described the peculiar radiant quality in van de Velde's landscapes as the 'Sunday atmosphere'. Few other painters were such close observers of the moist gleam of a meadow after rain or a wet green field in the rays of the setting sun.

This picture was acquired for the Berlin Gallery in 1899 from the collection of Lord Francis Pelham-Clinton-Hope in London. Bode's assumption that *The Farm* may have been intended as a companion-piece to *The Stag-hunt* now in the city museum in Frankfurt-on-Main seems dubious. On the other hand, both paintings have roughly the same dimensions and bear the date 1666.

248

JAN VERMEER VAN DELFT, 1632–1675
Lady and Gentleman drinking Wine. Canvas, 65 × 77 cm. Cat. No. 912 C.

A couple are shown sitting in a sparsely-furnished room, which is lit by a half-opened window. The man and woman, who have all the calm detachment of a still-life, have no apparent significance beyond their relationship to the objects around them, and the movement of the glass to the lips also has no ulterior meaning. There is nothing left to chance in this picture. The diagonally placed chair, on which a cushion, a lute and notebooks are lying, emphasizes the rectangular arrangement of the remaining furniture. It is the clarity of the room itself that Vermeer turns into a work of art.

The play of light, which patterns the grey walls with areas of brightness and half-shadow, is portrayed in masterly fashion and recalls the art of Rembrandt, but with the important difference that here it is introduced as an essential element of spatial co-ordination. In his use of colour, too, Vermeer achieved a quite unique and unmistakable effect: the colours are applied in such a way as to break up the light as if with glistening crystals, so allowing the contours to merge into the room. All the objects are bathed in a delicate shimmer of light, but without affecting their essential texture.

Vermeer presumably gained the technical training for his very particular use of light and his style of painting from the Rembrandt school, more especially in the person of the highly gifted Carel Fabritius, who was in Delft from 1650 to 1654. To judge by its style, the Berlin interior was painted *c.* 1660, when the artist was not yet thirty. Even Fabritius could not match the structural clarity and the artistic economy in the use of objects and colours; it is unparalleled in the whole range of Dutch painting.

This picture did not leave Delft until the eighteenth century, when it was put up for auction in 1736 (Jan van Loon). Later it found its way into the collection of Lord Francis Pelham-Clinton-Hope, from whom Bode acquired it in 1901 for the Berlin Gallery.

Jan Vermeer van Delft, 1632–1675
Young Lady with a Pearl Necklace. Canvas, 55 × 45 cm. Cat. No. 912 B.
Signed: J. v. Meer

The theme of the woman in front of a mirror is a common one in European painting
and has always been interpreted as symbolic of the transitory nature of life on earth.
As an allegorical expression of Christian ethics, it represented a fundamental Calvinist
trait in Dutch art. In fact, it is a subject that immediately evokes the 'Memento mori':
just as no one can hold fast the image in the mirror, so the earthly image of man is of
short duration. The pearl necklace and hair-ribbon, like the comb and powder-puff
on the table, are mere ornaments for the body, but when confronted with death, the
beautiful, finely-clad lady will not be measured by her outward appearance.

The yellow of the fur jacket and of the curtain, together with the grey of the wall,
provides the delicate colour-texture of this painting. Only the darker shade of the
crumpled cloth and of the porcelain vessel under the mirror is in striking contrast to
the figure caught in the light. She is wearing the only colourful object in the picture, a
red hair-ribbon.

The classical simplicity of the composition, which is largely rectangular, the simplicity
of the woman's profile and not least the solemnity of the atmosphere are all reminiscent
of a Grecian tomb-relief. Only the direction in which the subject is looking indicates
that it is a mirror that hangs on the wall before her. The brightly lit wall fills her entire
field of vision and provides the key necessary to interpret the meaning of her action.
Who, apart from Vermeer, has ever dared to make the grey expanse of a bare wall the
focal point of a picture?

Two decades after the painter's death this picture was auctioned in Amsterdam
(1696). Later it changed hands several times (Caudri auction 1809; Teengs auction
1811; Grevedon Collection; Bürger-Thoré Collection 1869), and finally reached the
Suermondt Collection, with which it was acquired for the Berlin Museum in 1874.

PIETER DE HOOCH, 1629–after 1683
The Mother. Canvas, 92 × 100 cm. Cat. No. 820B.

A young woman is sitting beside a cradle, lacing up her bodice. Behind her is an alcove with a partially drawn curtain, and on the wall above her head hang a brass warming-pan and a red dress. The light from a high window is diffused: at the back of the room, however, brighter light comes from an open door, where a small girl is looking out into the sunshine. The impression of depth in the picture seems quite natural but is very skilfully devised. The dog, which is looking back at the group in the foreground, draws the eye to both the child and the open door.

Pieter de Hooch, a native of Rotterdam, was an artist of very uneven quality. He produced his best works during a short period in Delft, when he was under the direct influence of Jan Vermeer's pictures; Vermeer was in this sense his teacher. The painting known by the title of *The Mother* was painted during this period, *c.* 1660, and somewhat later he produced the *Woman weighing Gold* (p. 289). The style of composition, which is built up almost like scaffolding and which seems to frame the figures, also occurs in Vermeer. But in contrast to him, Pieter de Hooch prefers a warmer range of colours, in which a deep red dominates, and he fills his interiors with soft light and golden tones. Pieter de Hooch's pictures radiate an atmosphere of tranquil well-being, which to this day has conditioned our image of Dutch interiors.

The painting was put up for auction in 1790 in Paris (M. Martin) and in 1827 in Haarlem (Hoffmann). Later it formed part of the Schneider Collection in Paris, where it was purchased in 1876 for the Picture Gallery.

GERARD TERBORCH, 1617–1681
The Paternal Admonition. Canvas, 70 × 60 cm. Cat. No. 791.

In the eighteenth century the subject of this painting was already something of a
mystery. A copper engraving by Johann Georg Wille bears the title 'The paternal
admonition', and even Goethe, who describes the painting in his *Wahlverwandschaften*
(*Elective Affinities*) adopted the erroneous explanation of the engraver. The real subject,
which is usually described euphemistically as the 'gallant offer', was highly popular in
Holland, particularly when, as in this case, the artist succeeded in cleverly disguising an
old theme. In fact, the presumed father, an officer, is offering the young woman a gold
coin; the alcove behind her and the objects on the table leave no doubt as to their
purpose. Mirror, comb and powder-puff were symbols of vanity, of the sinful life,
and the extinguished candle shows that the prospects are not good. While the seated
woman in the dark dress is clearly an intermediary, the scene culminates in the with-
holding movement of 'the splendid figure in the richly pleated, white satin dress'
(Goethe).

The figure with back turned to the viewer, thus concealing any expression of
emotion, is one of Terborch's favourite devices, which derives its effect from the
attraction of something concealed. His characters are almost always drawn from the
upper middle-class, which is detectable not so much in the environment as in the
clothes and gestures. Terborch was an unrivalled master in portraying silver-grey
silken material and he liked to contrast its metallic gleam with deep black and rich red.
It is an indication of the delicate and sober language of the painter, which satisfied the
wishes of a society that enjoyed a life of luxury, that, as tastes changed, the original
meaning of the picture was also forgotten.

The painting (of which another, rather different version is in the Rijksmuseum in
Amsterdam) must have been produced before 1655, as there is a copy by Caspar
Netscher in the Gotha Museum bearing this date.

The painting appears to have found its way to France in the course of the eighteenth
century. It was bought by Waagen in Paris in 1815 for the Picture Gallery.

JAN STEEN, 1626–1679
Outside an Inn. Canvas, 68 × 58 cm. Cat. No. 795.
Signed: J. Steen

Under the trees in the garden of an inn several guests have gathered to enjoy a meal. At a table in the foreground a mother is giving her child a drink. Opposite her sits a man, who is busy removing the scales from a herring. As he is looking straight from the canvas, it was believed at one time that this was the painter himself, particularly as Jan Steen for a time ran a brewery in Delft. But the self-portraits that have survived do not support this view.

After Rembrandt, Jan Steen was the outstanding painter of the city of Leyden. He left his birthplace at an early age and subsequently only lived there from time to time. His teachers were Nicolaus Knüpfer in Utrecht, Adriaen van Ostade in Haarlem and Jan van Goyen in The Hague. The last of these became his father-in-law in 1649. The various places in which he lived and worked are an indication of Jan Steen's creative unrest and the artistic roots of his œuvre. He spent almost ten years in Haarlem, after settling there *c.* 1660. This period seems to have been particularly fruitful and led to working relations with Haarlem artists. In the background of *The Christening* (p. 289) there appear two works by Frans Hals which must then have been in the artist's possession (cf. p. 230). This is not the only pointer to his relationship with the great master.

Jan Steen took his themes mostly from bourgeois or peasant family life. This work is reminiscent of Adriaen van Ostade's pictures of rural life. The well-balanced composition and unobtrusive way of telling a story make this picture one of the best and most appealing of the painter's works. The sensitive use of light and the muted colouring, in which only the red dress of the woman at the table predominates, are also features of painting by Pieter de Hooch, who undoubtedly knew Jan Steen in Delft.

In the royal palaces since the eighteenth century, the painting was transferred to the Picture Gallery in 1830.

Westphalian Master (beginning of the thirteenth century)
Altarpiece with scenes from the Passion

Westphalian Master (*c.* 1250–70) *Altarpiece with the Holy Trinity*

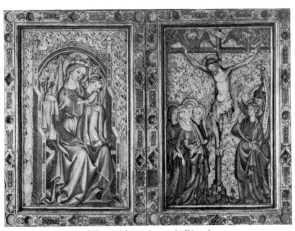

Cologne Master (*c.* 1350) *Diptych*

Master of the Lower Rhine *Joseph recognizes Mary as the Mother of Christ*

261

Bohemian Master (c. 1370) *The Nativity*

Bohemian Master (c. 1360)
Christ on the Cross

Master of the Upper Rhine (c. 1400)
The Nativity

Hans Multscher *Christ carrying the Cross*

Hans Multscher *The Adoration of the Magi*

Konrad Witz *The Queen of Sheba
before Solomon*

Master of the Life of the Virgin
The Virgin and Child with Female Saints

Master of the Darmstadt Passion
The Adoration of the Magi and *The Virgin enthroned*

Master of the Housebook
Christ washing the Feet of the Disciples

Upper German Master (end of the fifteenth century)
The Martyrdom of Saint Sebastian

Hans Holbein the Elder
The Virgin Mourning

Albrecht Dürer
Portrait of Frederick the Wise

Lucas Cranach the Elder
Venus and Cupid

Lucas Cranach the Elder
Portrait of Frau Reuss

263

Albrecht Dürer
Portrait of a Young Girl

Albrecht Dürer
Portrait of Jacob Muffel

Albrecht Dürer
Portrait of a Young Woman

Christoph Amberger *Portrait of
the Cosmographer Sebastian Münster*

Albrecht Dürer
The Virgin at Prayer

Hans Süss von Kulmbach
Portrait of a Young Man

Hans Baldung Grien
Pyramus and Thisbe

Hans Baldung Grien
The Virgin and Child with St John

Hans Baldung Grien
The Adoration of the Magi

Albrecht Altdorfer
The Nativity

Albrecht Altdorfer
Christ on the Cross

Wolf Huber *The Flight into Egypt*

Master of Messkirch *The Lamentation*

Lucas Cranach the Younger *The Fountain of Youth*

265

Hans Holbein the Younger
*Portrait of Duke Anton
of Lorraine*

Hans Holbein the Younger
*Portrait of Hermann
Hillebrandt Wedigh*

Hans Holbein the Younger *Man with a Lute*

Netherlandish Master (*c.* 1390) *Triptych*

French Master (*c.* 1400) *Diptych*

French Master (*c.* 1400)
The Coronation of the Virgin

Simon Marmion *St Omer Altarpiece* (left and right wings)

Master of Flémalle
The Madonna of Humility

Master of Flémalle
Christ on the Cross

Jan van Eyck
Portrait of Baudouin de Lannoy

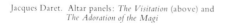

Petrus Christus. Altar wings: *The Annunciation and the Nativity*
and *The Last Judgment*

Jacques Daret. Altar panels: *The Visitation* (above) and
The Adoration of the Magi

268

Jan van Eyck *Man with Carnations*

Master of Flémalle
Portrait of a Stout Man

Rogier van der Weyden
Portrait of Charles the Bold

Rogier van der Weyden *Altarpiece of St John the Baptist*

Rogier van der Weyden
The Lamentation

Geertgen tot Sint Jans
The Virgin and Child

Hugo van der Goes
The Lamentation

Gerard David
The Crucifixion

Hans Memling
The Virgin and Child

Gerard David *The Virgin and Child*

Michel Sittow *The Virgin and Child*

Joos van Cleve
Portrait of a Young Man

Willem Key
Portrait of a Young Man

Master of the Mansi Magdalene
Mary Magdalene

Quinten Massys
The Virgin and Child enthroned

Jan Gossaert *The Virgin and Child*

Lucas van Leyden *The Virgin
and Child with Angels*

Jan Gossaert
Portrait of a Nobleman

Jan van Scorel
Portrait of a Young Man

Maerten van Heemskerck *The Baptism of Christ*

Joachim Patinir *The Rest on the Flight into Egypt*

Jan Sanders van Hemessen *A Merry Company*

Pieter Aertsen
Market Woman at a Vegetable Stall

Pieter Bruegel the Elder *Netherlandish Proverbs*

Tuscan Master (*c.* 1270)
The Virgin and Child enthroned

Maso di Banco
Madonna and Child

Florentine Master (*c.* 1330)
The Miracle of the Girdle

Taddeo Gaddi *Altarpiece (triptych)*

Giotto di Bondone *The Crucifixion*

Bernardo Daddi *Altarpiece (triptych)*

Allegretto Nuzi *Diptych*

Sienese Master (*c.* 1360)
The Annunciation

Lippo Memmi
The Virgin and Child (Cat. 1067)

Lippo Memmi
The Virgin and Child (Cat. 1072)

Ugolino da Siena *The Scourging of Christ*

Giovanni di Paolo *The Crucifixion*

Pietro Lorenzetti *The Blessed Humilitas heals a Sick Nun*

Gentile da Fabriano
The Virgin enthroned with two Saints

Fra Angelico
The Virgin and Child enthroned

Fra Angelico *The Last Judgment*

Masaccio *Lying-in Room of a
Florentine Lady*

Masaccio *Four Saints*

Masaccio *The Adoration of the Magi*

275

Piero della Francesca
St Jerome Penitent

Domenico Veneziano
The Martyrdom of Saint Lucy

Pesellino *The Crucifixion*

Antonio del Pollaiuolo
David as Victor

Piero del Pollaiuolo *The Annunciation*

Domenico Ghirlandaio
Judith with her Maidservant

Andrea del Verrocchio
The Virgin and Child

Lorenzo di Credi
Portrait of a Young Girl

Fra Filippo Lippi
Portrait of a Lady

Luca Signorelli. Wings of an altarpiece, each
showing three angels

Botticelli *The Virgin enthroned
with two Saints*

Botticelli
Portrait of Giuliano de' Medici

Botticelli
Portrait of a Young Man

Botticelli *Portrait of a Young
Woman (Simonetta Vespucci?)*

Botticelli *Venus*

Filippino Lippi *Allegory of Music*

Jacopino del Conte
Portrait of a Man

Raphael *The Virgin and Child with two Saints*

Raphael *Madonna di Casa Colonna*

Raphael *The Virgin and Child*

Franciabigio *Portrait of a Young Man*

Bronzino *Portrait of Eleanor of Toledo*

Rosso Fiorentino *Portrait of a Young Man*

Mantegna *The Presentation of Christ in the Temple*

Mantegna *Portrait of Cardinal Lodovico Mezzarota*

Bartolommeo Montagna
The Risen Christ with Saints

Carlo Crivelli *The Virgin enthroned
with seven Saints*

Giovanni Bellini
The Virgin and Child

Cima da Conegliano
The Virgin and Child with Donor

Antonello da Messina
Portrait of a Young Man (Cat. 18 A)

Cima da Conegliano
The Healing of Anianus

Cima da Conegliano *The Virgin
enthroned with four Saints*

Giovanni Bellini
The Resurrection

Titian *Girl with a Bowl of Fruit*

Titian *Self-portrait*

Cariani *Reclining Woman in a Landscape*

Giovanni Girolamo Savoldo
A Venetian Lady

Lorenzo Lotto *Christ taking
leave of his Mother*

Vittore Carpaccio *The Ordination of St Stephen*

Tintoretto *The Virgin and
Child on the Crescent Moon*

Veronese *The Dead Christ*

El Greco *Mater Dolorosa*

Velázquez *Three Musicians*

Spanish Master (first half of seventeenth century) *Still-life
with Books, Inkstand and Hour-glass*

Giovanni Baglione
Sacred and Profane Love

Bartolomé Estéban Murillo
The Baptism of Christ

Francisco de Zurbarán *Portrait of
a Youth of Noble Birth*

281

Carlo Maratti
Portrait of a Young Man

Guercino *The Marriage of
St Catherine*

Agostino Carracci *Portrait of
Giovanna Parolini-Guicciardini*

Louis Le Nain
The Adoration of the Shepherds

Nicolas Poussin *Helios and Phaeton*

Nicolas Poussin *The Nurture of Jupiter*

Simon Vouet *The Toilet of Venus*

Bernardo Strozzi
Judith with the Head of Holofernes

Giovanni Battista Tiepolo *Rinaldo in the Garden of Armida*

Giovanni Battista Piazzetta
St John the Baptist

Giovanni Battista Tiepolo *Christ carrying the Cross*

Giovanni Battista Tiepolo
Pan and Syrinx

Canaletto *The Church of S. Maria Salute in Venice*

Antoine Watteau *The Garden Party*

Antoine Pesne
The Artist and his Daughters

Jean François de Troy *Breakfast*

Antoine Watteau *The Italian Comedy*

John Zoffany *A Married Couple*

Thomas Gainsborough
Portrait of Mrs Robert Hingeston

284

Peter Paul Rubens *Landscape with the Shipwreck of Aeneas*

Jacob Jordaens *The Return of the Holy Family from Egypt*

Peter Paul Rubens
Portrait of Isabella Brant

Peter Paul Rubens *Landscape with a Tower*

Peter Paul Rubens
Andromeda chained to the Rock

Sir Anthony van Dyck
Portrait of a Genoese Gentleman

Sir Anthony van Dyck
The Marchesa Geronima Spinola

Cornelis de Vos *The Artist's Children*

David Teniers the Younger
The Artist with his Wife and Son

Esaias van de Velde *View of Zierikzee*

Willem Pietersz Buytewech *A Merry Party*

Hercules Seghers *Dutch Landscape near Rhenen*

Frans Hals
Portrait of a Young Man

Frans Hals
Portrait of a Young Woman

Frans Hals
Singing Boy with a Flute

Frans Hals *Portrait of Tyman Oosdorp*

Salomon van Ruysdael *Landscape with Sailing Boats*

Philips Wouwerman *Winter Landscape*

Jan van Goyen *View of Arnhem*

Rembrandt *Self-portrait with Iron Collar*

Rembrandt *The Artist's Wife Saskia*

Rembrandt *The Money-changer*

Pieter Pietersz Lastman *Susannah and the Elders*

Rembrandt *The Vision of Daniel*

Rembrandt *Joseph and Potiphar's Wife*

Aert de Gelder *The Holy Family*

Rembrandt *Jacob wrestling with the Angel*

Gerard Terborch *The Concert*

Pieter de Hooch *Woman weighing Gold*

Jan Steen *The Christening*

Aert van der Neer *Winter Landscape*

Philips Koninck *Dutch Landscape*

Adriaen van de Velde *Landscape with grazing Horses*

Meindert Hobbema
Road between Groups of Trees and Farm-houses

Jacob van Ruisdael *View of Haarlem*

Gabriel Metsu *The Sick Woman*

Willem Kalf *Still-life with Glass
Goblet and Fruit*

Barent Fabritius *Slaughtered Pig*

LIST OF ILLUSTRATIONS

Numbers in italics indicate reproductions in colour.

296

INDEX

Numbers in italics refer to the illustrations.